THE FLUTE BENEATH THE GOLD

To Mercer University

The Flute Beneath the Gold

READING THE BIBLE AND SPEAKING THE TRUTH

by Charles E. Poole

SMYTH&HELWYS
PUBLISHING, INCORPORATED   MACON, GEORGIA

Smyth & Helwys Publishing, Inc.
6316 Peake Road
Macon, Georgia 31210-3960
1-800-747-3016
©2002 by Smyth & Helwys Publishing
All rights reserved.
Printed in the United States of America.

The paper used in this publication meets the min-
imum requirements of American National
Standard for Information Sciences—Permanence
of Paper for Printed Library Materials.
ANSI Z39.48–1984. (alk. paper)

Library of Congress Cataloging-in-Publication Data

Poole, Charles E.
        The flute beneath the gold : reading the Bible and speaking the truth/
        Charles E. Poole.
                p. cm.
        Includes bibliographical references.
        ISBN 1-57312-360-9 (pbk)
        1. Bible—Theology.
        2. Bible—Sermons.
        3. Baptists—Sermons
        4. Sermons, American—20th century.
        I. Title

        BS543 .P66 2002
        232'.041—dc21

                                                        2001057610
                                                        CIP

Contents

Preface

When I was a boy, my most high-tech possession (next to my electric guitar with the reverb lever) was a plastic transistor radio that used those rectangular, nine-volt "Black Cat" batteries. I was listening to it in awe on that autumn day when Sandy Koufax refused to pitch in a World Series game because it fell on Yom Kippur. I was listening to it in wonder the Friday night my hometown hero Riley Bennett scored five touchdowns in one game for old Lanier High School in Macon, Georgia. And I always listened to it in reverence when the "Back to the Bible" broadcast came on, with its invitation for all of us out in Radioland to climb aboard "The Bible Bus."

Parts of this book have left me feeling like a token-taker on the Bible bus, recruting riders for a journey "back to the Bible." That, of course, is not a non-stop route. You can't go straight from Atlanta to Antioch or Nashville to Nazareth. There is no non-stop ticket from Dallas to Damascus or Jackson to Jerusalem, not even on the Bible bus. What has happened in the past twenty centuries of evolving Christianity cannot be ignored, nor should it be. The creeds, the doctrines, the organized, institutionalized, denominationalized church—they are all important structures for the practice of our faith. There can never be any non-stop "back to the Bible" journey that bypasses the traditions that have emerged to guide our lives, nor should there be. (Indeed, the Bible itself is the product of a process of canonization that spanned the church's earliest centuries.) But, having said that, I do believe that people who are serious about God and the gospel need to read the whole Bible and speak the truth about what we find there, even if that truth doesn't always exactly echo the doctrines and dogma that have emerged over the centuries.

This book's central idea might best be captured in a simple question for which there is no easy answer: *If we read the whole Bible and speak the truth about what we find there, how does that match up with the conventional wisdom of standard, official Christianity as it has evolved across the centuries?* Other pastoral questions are raised in these pages (having to do with such matters as prayer, the brevity of life, and the mystery of suffering) but that question is the recurring theme. An honest struggle to answer that question would suggest that sometimes, reading the Bible and speaking the truth will make one seem conservative about "orthodox Christianity." Sometimes, it will make one seem liberal. In either case, neither matters. What matters only and always is that we trust God's grace, seek God's will, speak God's truth, embody God's spirit, share God's love, and live the life to which God has called us.

The words that are traveling in this book are collected as essays. I use the word "essay" here in the earliest sense of the word, back when "essay" was less a noun and more a verb, a verb that meant "to try" or "to make an effort." Here are words that are tries at the truth, good faith efforts at speaking the truth about a few of the many corners where Scripture intersects life. Thus they are, in the oldest sense of the word, essays; efforts, attempts, tries at the truth.

Most of the words that reside inside the walls of this book had earlier attempts as sermons in a pulpit or lectures on a campus. Invitations to speak at the Baptist Theological Seminary at Richmond, the Baptist House of Studies at Duke Divinity School, and the Furman University Pastors' School all prodded me to ponder much of what has fermented into this book. For those kind invitations I thank Charles Bugg at Richmond, Furman Hewitt at Duke, and Jim Pitts at Furman. I also wish to thank Smyth and Helwys Publishing Company for bringing these words to the light of day. I express my gratitude to Shirley Sanders Reid for her patient typing of my handwritten words through their many revisions.

Always I am thankful for Northminster Baptist Church, a remarkable family of faith in which to think and worship and pray and sing and grow. Most of all I am thankful for Marcia, Joshua, and Maria. Whatever clarity these words have acquired is largely due to the lively conversations we have had around the house across the years.

This gathering of devotional essays is dedicated to Mercer University, with gratitude for a lifetime of learning.

Charles E. Poole
Jackson, Mississippi
The Season of Pentecost, 2001

The Flute Beneath the Gold

"I believe that God is far less squeamish than are God's theological bodyguards."[1] That memorable old line from the wonderful Quaker Douglas Steere came wandering up next to me one day as I walked and prayed and gazed up into a hazy July sky. Walking and praying, I found myself asking God something like this: "What really is the truth, God? I know what your most well-intentioned doctrinal bodyguards say we should believe. I know what organized religion says we must believe. But what, God, is the truth; the unvarnished, unadorned truth, the truth about heaven and hell, about how conversion occurs, about what the church was originally intended to be, about Judaism and Christianity and other faiths and who's in the kingdom and who's not?" Walking and praying, I found myself asking those unaskable questions, wondering about that part of the truth we cannot ever fully know; the truth beneath, beyond, and behind all the protective layers within which organized religion wraps the gospel of God.

Some would dismiss such inquiries into the truth as just so much silliness because, after all, anyone who wishes to know the truth can find the truth easily enough by reading the Bible.

Those who would say such a thing have a point, of course. We do find the truth that matters most in the Bible; but the Bible, as inspired and inspiring as it is, does not speak with one voice but many, which means that much of the Bible's truth most often comes to us wrapped in a layer of interpretation that chooses one Bible verse over another. For example, in one place, the Bible says that Jesus "has abolished the law" (Eph 2:15) but in another place, the same Bible quotes Jesus as saying, "Do not think that I have come to abolish the law" (Matt 5:17). In one place, the Bible suggests a small remnant will make it into life everlasting: "The gate is narrow and the road is hard that leads to life, and there are few who find it" (Matt 7:14), while in another place, the same Bible portrays vast throngs who make it in: "After this I looked, and there was a great multitude no one could count, from every nation, from all tribes and people and languages, standing before the throne and before the lamb, robed in white.... These are they who have come out of the great ordeal; they have washed their robes and made them white in the blood of the Lamb" (Rev 7:9, 14). None of this is to suggest that the Bible is a chaotic collection of contradictions. To the contrary, the Bible is inspired, inspiring, powerful, and wonderful. But if one reads the Bible and speaks the truth, one has to confess that the Bible does speak with many voices, a fact that requires interpretation, and that leaves us always with someone's interpretative conclusions standing between us and the unvarnished truth we seek to know.

Some would say that is precisely where the truth (as much truth as we need to know) should be found—in the interpretative conclusions that reside in the creeds and doctrines of the church. "Who are we," some would ask, "to question the conclusions of the wise ones who constructed the creeds and defined the doctrines?" But remember who decided on the doctrines and codified the creeds—ordinary people like you and me, complex human beings who happened to be bishops but who were, fundamentally, exactly what we are, sinners saved by grace and seeking truth. Who is to say that their conclusions about God and the gospel were somehow more accurate than any other sincere seekers' conclusions? I say that, not to suggest that their conclusions (and thus, our creeds) are flawed or mistaken, but to suggest that if we are going to invest the official doctrines of the church with the authority to say what Christians must believe, then we at least need to know, and say out loud, that those doctrines were arrived at by real human beings involved in human proceedings that produced the creeds and dogma to which Christians now pledge our faith.

There may be no clearer example of that than the doctrines that have emerged to define the relationship between Jesus and God. The question of who Jesus is in relation to God was the great issue that prompted the convening of the church councils at Nicea in AD 325, at Ephesus in 431, and at Chalcedon in 451. The council at Nicea was convened by the emperor Constantine to squelch the growing unrest fermenting around a vigorous debate over the relationship between Jesus and God. The principal figures in the debate were Alexander, the Bishop of Alexandria; and Arius, a leading churchman in Alexandria. Arius accused Alexander of abandoning monotheism because Alexander made Christ co-eternal and co-equal with God, which in Arius' mind left Alexander too close to having two gods, one called "God" and one called "Christ." Alexander accused Arius of abandoning the divinity of Christ, because Arius saw Christ as created by God, thus coming after God — God's unique Son, but not God's co-eternal equal. Their debate became so divisive and public (including demonstrations in the streets!) that Constantine called for a gathering of bishops at Nicea to settle the matter. The bishops (some say about three hundred were present) sided with Alexander's view and denounced Arius as a heretic because, though he confessed Christ as the Son of God, he made too much of a distinction between Christ and God. The bishops' conclusions were codified in the Nicene Creed, which responded to Arius' heresy by saying that Jesus is "God of God" and "true God of true God." That became orthodox Christian doctrine by vote of the bishops who met at Nicea by order of the emperor.

The creed those bishops adopted was, and is, beautiful, powerful, and instructive. But, if we read the Bible and speak the truth about what we read, what we find is that there are as many Bible verses that Arius might have turned to in support of a clear distinction between Jesus and God as there are that the bishops might have cited in support of the "orthodox" view that Jesus is "true God of true God." By my count, there are twenty-six places in the New Testament that seem to say "Jesus is God":

> Matthew 1:23; John 1:1-3, 5:44, 8:19, 8:58, 10:31-33,
> 12:45, 14:7-9, 17:21-22, 20:28; Acts 7:59, 9:34, 16:7;
> Philippians 2:5-6, Colossians 1:15-17, 1:19, 2:9;
> Hebrews 1:3, 1:8; 1 Timothy 6:13-16; Titus 1:3-4, 2:13,
> 3:4-6; 2 Peter 1:1; Revelation 17:14 and 19:16.

Among the most powerful of those are these: 2 Peter 1:1, which uses the phrase "Our God and Savior Jesus Christ," and Titus 2:13, which also speaks of "our great God and Savior, Jesus Christ." Then there is Paul's great hymn in Philippians 2, which says of Jesus that "he was in the form of God [and] did not regard equality with God as something to be exploited." Another major voice for the idea that there is no distinction between Jesus and God is found in Colossians: "In Christ all the fullness of God was pleased to dwell" (Col 1:9). And then there are the verses from John, most notably John 1:1, "In the beginning was the Word, and the Word was with God and the Word was God"; John 8:58, "If you knew me you would know my Father also"; John 10:30, "The Father and I are one"; and, of course, John 14:9, "Whoever has seen me has seen the Father." There are twenty-six such passages in the New Testament. They form the basis for the theological idea that "Jesus is God," the idea embodied in The Nicene Creed that was adopted in opposition to Arius.

If those twenty-six Bible passages were the only verses we had, that would be that. But if we actually read the Bible and speak the truth, there is more to say. Living in the same New Testament with those twenty-six passages that seem to make no distinction between Jesus and God are forty passages that seem to make a real distinction between Jesus and God. Here they are:

> Matthew 3:17, 16:16-17, 17:5; Mark 1:1, 1:11, 9:7, 10:18, 14:35-36; Luke 3:22, 6:12, 9:35, 18:19, 23:46; John 1:18, 3:16, 4:34, 5:19, 5:30, 6:38, 7:16-17, 8:40-42, 12:44 & 49, 13:3, 17:3, 20:17; Acts 2:22 & 24, 3:13, 13:32; Romans 8:32; Galatians 4:4; Colossians 1:3, 1 Thessalonians 1:9-10; Hebrews 1:1-2, 5:5-9, 9:14 & 24, 10:7, 13:20; 1 Timothy 2:5; 1 John 4:9-10, 12 & 14-15; 1 Peter 1:21.

Significant among those verses are these: "No one has ever seen God.... God abides in those who confess that Jesus is the Son of God" (1 John 4:12 & 15); and "Jesus spent the night in prayer to God" (Luke 6:12). In Luke 18:19, Jesus, in response to a compliment, said, "Why do you call me good? No one is good but God alone." And then there is John 8:40 and 42, where Jesus says, "Now you are trying to kill me, a man who has told you the truth that I heard from God.... I came from God.... I did not come on my own, but God sent me." And in John 13:3, there is this: "Jesus, knowing that he had come from God and was going to God, got up from the table."

What are we to do with all this? In the same Bible are verses that make no distinction between Jesus and God alongside verses that speak of Jesus praying to God, coming from God, going to God, and differentiating himself from God. The Council at Nicea homogenized all those various voices into a creed that declared Jesus to be "true God of true God." The creed is powerful, beautiful, and enduring. It is an abiding guide for our lives in the church. But if we read the Bible and speak the truth, we have to say that Arius, whose heresy the creed was written to squelch, could have garnered as many Bible verses to support a distinction between Jesus and God as the orthodox victors could have enlisted in support of their conclusion that Jesus was not only the Son of God, but "true God of true God."

That doesn't mean that Arius was right and the creed is wrong. (Indeed, Arius had some very strange ideas.[2] The creed probably landed nearer the truth than Arius.) But it is a clear example of the fact that the Bible itself is not nearly as neat and tidy and manageable as the doctrines that have been wrapped around the gospel of God, layer upon layer, across twenty centuries of Christianity. We need to know that, lest we blindly embrace as gospel that which has been wrapped around the gospel by the gospel's well-meaning defenders.

All of this calls to mind that old fable about Moses' flute. As the legend goes, in the days when Moses worked as a shepherd, he carried a simple wooden flute on which he played a tune to call the sheep. After Moses died, according to the story, the flute became prized as a holy relic from the life of the great leader. Eventually, those who wished to preserve Moses' flute had it covered in layers of gold. Once it was gold-plated, the flute certainly looked more sacred and seemed more special, but, covered in all those layers of gold, it no longer made the music for which it was created.[3]

The legend of Moses' flute strikes me as a parable of all those well-intentioned layers that have been added to the original music of the gospel of God. The simple truth that God sent Jesus to reveal has become weighed down with the accumulated layers of twenty centuries of evolving Christianity. That doesn't mean that the added layers of creed, dogma, doctrine, and denomination are bad or wrong. They can, in fact, be good and helpful guides and structures for the practice of our faith. But we at least need to understand that some of what we embrace as standard, conventional, "official" Christianity was wrapped around the original gospel by those who were trying to guard and protect it, not unlike the gold that got wrapped around Moses' flute.

What if we could peel back some of those layers, look behind them and find our way back to the flute beneath the gold, the gospel without the guards? I know it isn't that simple. We can't just "get back to the Bible." And we mustn't just retreat to our rooms with a Bible in our hands to arrive at "our own individual interpretation." The fact is, we all will always read Scripture and seek truth through the acquired lens of Christian history and church doctrine, and we need the church to guide us in that quest. But if we could at least read the Bible, actually read all of it, and then speak the truth about what we have found, perhaps we could recover some simpler song; some less-encumbered tune that waits somewhere near the faraway place where the gold ends and the flute begins.

Amen.

* * * * *

In his book *The Silence of Jesus*, James Breech recalls going to hear W. H. Auden read some of his poetry at Princeton years ago. The lecture hall was jammed, he says, with hundreds of people all chattering with excitement. When the old man finally came out on the stage to read, he read in a voice so soft that even the microphone did not help. People immediately began whispering to each other what they thought Auden had said until the poet himself could no longer be heard. His would-be interpreters had drowned him out. What Breech learned that night, he says, is that…"In order for the speaker's own voice to be heard, the go-betweens must be silent."

When the poet happens to be God, this advice takes on special significance.

—*Barbara Brown Taylor,* When God Is Silent

NOTES

[1] Douglas V. Steere, *Dimensions of Prayer* (Nashville: Upper Room Books, 1997), 55.

[2] One of the most interesting treatments of Arius and the Council at Nicea is Richard E. Rubenstein's *When Jesus Became God* (San Diego: Harcourt, 1999).

[3] Leslie D. Weatherhead, *The Christian Agnostic* (Nashville: Abingdon Press, 1965), 27.

CHAPTER ONE

Central Standard Time

I therefore, the prisoner in the Lord, beg you to lead a life worthy of the calling to which you have been called, with all humility and gentleness, with patience, bearing with one another in love, making every effort to maintain the unity of the Spirit in the bond of peace. There is one body and one Spirit, just as you were called to the one hope of your calling, one Lord, one faith, one baptism, one God and Father of all, who is above all and through all and in all . . .

We must no longer be children, tossed to and fro and blown about by every wind of doctrine, by people's trickery, by their craftiness in deceitful scheming. But speaking the truth in love, we must grow up in every way into him who is the head, into Christ, from whom the whole body, joined and knit together by every ligament with which it is equipped, as each part is working properly, promotes the body's growth in building itself up in love.

—Ephesians 4:1-6, 14-16

> One of the scribes came near . . . and asked Jesus,
> "Which commandment is the first of all?"
>
> —*Mark 12:28*

Ephesians chapter four recites a list of seven wonderful "ones": One body, one Spirit, one hope, one Lord, one faith, one baptism, one God. If only there was one more "one"; an eighth one. Then perhaps the list would go like this: "There is one body, one Spirit, one hope, one Lord, one faith, one baptism, one God . . . *and one opinion!*" If only there was one opinion, one perspective, one interpretation concerning the meaning and purpose and mission of the one body, the one Spirit, the one hope, the one Lord, the one faith, the one baptism, or even the one God. But, of course, it is not so. There may be one Lord, one faith, and one baptism, but there is far more than one opinion about what those great realities give to us and demand from us.

It seems that there was more than one opinion in Ephesus, because the letter writer's great plea in Ephesians 4 is for unity: "I beg you to lead a life worthy of the calling to which you have been called . . . bearing with one another in love, making every effort to maintain the unity of the Spirit in the bond of peace." Apparently, opposing opinions and conflicting perspectives troubled the Ephesian congregation, prompting this urgent call for unity and peace.

But, as important as unity and peace are to the writer of Ephesians, they are not to be bought at the price of the truth. In Ephesians 4:14 and 15, the writer says, "We must no longer be children, tossed to and fro by every wind of doctrine . . . . But speaking the truth in love, we must grow up in every way into Christ." The writer of Ephesians knows that the truth must never be sacrificed on the altar of agreeableness. There is no grace in dishonesty and no dishonesty in grace, so despite his longing for unity in Ephesus, the writer pleads for unity based on speaking the truth.

Of course, the problem is that everyone who has an opinion sincerely believes that they *are* speaking the truth. So, how do you know which of the conflicting perspectives is true? When it is time to "speak the truth in love," how does one discern what that "truth" is? Well, the simple answer of much conventional Christianity is, "I go by the Book. I let the Bible decide for me what is truth and what isn't truth." That's a fine answer, and you can say that with integrity once you live by it. Once you don't own more than one coat (Luke 3:10), once you give to everyone who begs from you and loan to everyone who asks of you (Matt 5:42), once you wear no jewelry and visit no salon (1 Tim 2:9). Once you begin actually to live by the words in the Bible, then you can say that you go by the Book, that the Bible is your standard for truth. But in the meantime, all any of us can honestly say is that the Bible *as we interpret it* is the standard by which we decide what is, and is not, the truth among competing opinions.

Once we've said that, then we're ready for the real question: "*By what central standard do we interpret Scripture?*" That standard finally determines our opinions, our convictions, and our perspectives on life's questions, dilemmas, and issues. We all have an opinion about what the truth is. That is not the kind of opinion we are free to think up on our own. We don't get to just make up our own mind about all this. Our mind is to be formed by the truth of Scripture and the teaching of a family of faith, a community of believers, a congregation. But the fact is, what we finally embrace as fundamentally important and ultimately true will be colored and shaped by some central standard by which we judge things to be true or untrue, important or unimportant. So, what is your central standard?

Once, when someone asked Jesus what his central standard for life was, Jesus replied by saying, "Love the Lord your God with all that is in you and love others as much as you love your own self." That is the central standard, according to Jesus, by which we must live all of life. According to Jesus, that is the truth greater, higher, and deeper than all other truth; the fundamental, irreducible, central standard of life; the last court of appeal in tough cases, close calls, hard questions, moral quandaries, and ethical dilemmas. In the face of a multitude of sincerely held opinions, ideas, and perspectives, we need a standard that is the central truth against which to measure all of our many opinions, some overriding reality that finally tilts us one way or the other. You need to know what your central standard is and how you chose it, because it is probably the single most dependable predictor for how you will respond to problems, to people, and to issues.

There is One God, One Lord, One Faith, One Hope, One Gospel, and ultimately, finally, when we die, we are all going to know what the One Truth that mattered really was. In the meantime, we form opinions, hold convictions, embrace doctrines, and have ideas—all of which grow out of some deep, fundamental, central standard that rings truest to us at the center of our soul. When we face life's murky dilemmas and hard choices, when we have to decide which way to go on ethical questions and social issues for which there is no clear path, it is time to be guided by our central standard.

Jesus knew what his was, and he lived by it. And died by it.

Amen.

* * * * *

Opinions may be mistaken, but love never is.

—*Harry Emerson Fosdick*

CHAPTER TWO

How Do You Pick and Choose?

When the Pharisees heard that he had silenced the Sadducees,
they gathered, and one of them, a lawyer, asked him a question
to test him. "Teacher, which commandment in the law is the
greatest?"

He said to him, "'You shall love the Lord your God with all
your heart, and with all your soul, and with all your mind.' This
is the greatest and first commandment. And a second is like it:
'You shall love your neighbor as yourself.' On these two commandments hang all the law and the prophets."

—Matthew 22:34-40

When it comes to the Bible, how do you do your picking and
choosing? When you're picking the parts of the Bible by which
you will actually live, how do you make those choices? Now,
there's not much point in wasting time protesting that we don't
pick and choose. It's a nice thought, but it won't stand up to the
hard light of day. It is an inarguable fact that people interpret
Scripture. The book of Deuteronomy, for example, is in the
Bible. Deuteronomy 21:21 provides for the stoning of stubborn
children. We don't do that, nor should we. The book of Numbers

is also in the Bible. Numbers 15:35 says that God instructed Moses to execute a man who was found picking up sticks on the Sabbath. We find that unthinkable, as we should. Even people fond of the phrase "inerrant infallible Bible" don't assign abiding authority to these Bible verses. *"Well, sure but, that's the Old Testament."*

So, one could say that we Christians pick and choose which Bible verses will govern and guide us on the basis of our preference for the New Testament. But that doesn't quite resolve the issue. For example, the New Testament book of 1 Timothy says that women should keep silent in the church, but the equally New Testament book of Galatians says that in the church there is neither male nor female. One verse in 1 Corinthians 14 says that women should not lead in worship, but another verse in 1 Corinthians 11 offers a dress code for women worship leaders. Both Corinthian passages are in the New Testament. So how people decide, for example, on the question of the role of women in the church is obviously based on some sort of picking and choosing that has nothing to do with a New Testament preference over the Old Testament.

We might like to say, *"When it comes to the Bible, I would never pick and choose. I live by it all."* But the fact is, we can't say that and speak the truth. No one can. The question is not, "Do we pick and choose?" The only real question is, "How do we pick and choose?" By what measure do we decide which Scripture will guide our lives, shape our opinions, and govern our actions?

For me, the answer to that question goes something like this: I begin with what I believe to be the most basic, fundamental Christian confession: The life of Jesus is the best revelation of God ever seen by the world. So, if Jesus is our best look at God, then my best hope to know how God wants me to live is to learn as much as I can about Jesus. And where do I go to learn about Jesus? To the place where the words and works of Jesus are recorded; which is, of course, the four gospels. So, I read the four gospels over and over again, saturating my mind with the words and works of Jesus, and I then strive to let the spirit of Jesus as revealed in the four gospels become the standard by which I interpret the rest of the Bible.

Of course, it's not always that simple. For one thing, there are so many matters to which Jesus never spoke, at least as far as we can know. In those cases, you just have to read the four gospels over and over again until you develop a feel for the spirit of Christ that you can call on in the face of life's complex questions and difficult issues. That can be complicated, and sometimes it can become pretty subjective. When it comes to the issues of the day to which Jesus never spoke, we tend to interpret Scripture in the light of our own worldview. We especially want the Bible to support our politics and our economics. It's hard to read the Bible without that subjective lens, especially when we're trying to find "the Jesus position" on issues Jesus never mentioned.

But that's not the worst problem we face when we try to read the Bible with Jesus as our measure of truth. The worst problem is not trying to discern "the Jesus position" on matters Jesus never mentioned. The worst problem is trying to obey the Jesus position on matters Jesus did mention! That's the truly hard part. The worst problem is not where Jesus left no clear directions. The worst problem is where Jesus left crystal clear instructions. For example, what do we do with the gospel's most radical words? "Love your enemies. Do good to those who hate you. Give to everyone who begs from you. Loan, expecting nothing in return. If someone takes your coat, give them your shirt." And then, perhaps hardest of all, there is this: "Be merciful to one another, even as God is merciful to you." What do we do with such a "radical Jesus" Scripture passage? We can't just pick and choose our way around it, because what it says is at the heart of the gospel. But how do we know that? If I say this passage is central to the gospel, aren't I picking and choosing? On what basis do I pick this passage as more central than some other passage?

7

Well, I go back to the passage that, for me, is the hinge on which the rest of the Bible turns, Matthew 22:34-40, where an inquirer asks Jesus which commandment is the most important of all. Now, obviously, Jesus could have responded by saying that all Bible verses are of equal authority, all Scriptures are of equal significance, and all of God's commandments are of equal importance. He had his chance to say that. But that is not what Jesus said. Jesus said, "The greatest commandment is this, 'You shall love the Lord your God with all your heart and with all your soul and with all your mind.' And the second greatest is this, 'Love your neighbor as yourself.'"

Now, if you believe, as I do, that the gospels are a trustworthy record of the life of Jesus, then there's the last court of appeal for biblical picking and choosing. If Jesus is the central measure of our Christian faith, then the gospels that record his words are the central measure of all Scripture for Christians. In those gospels, Jesus said that the central standard of life is this: "Love God with all that is in you and love others as you love yourself." That's how I know that when I stumble across a passage that demands radical, life-altering, world-changing love for all other people, I am at the irreducible center of the gospel. If I pick and choose my way around this radical center of the gospel, "Love your enemies. Give to all who beg from you. Be merciful to all as God is merciful to all," then my picking and choosing, which at other times may be a necessary virtue, becomes a sin against the heart and soul of the gospel of God.

Amen.

* * * * *

For Christians, the dialogue between God and God's people found its fullest expression in Christ, and so Christ became the key to the whole of Scripture.

—*Rowan Greer*
Early Biblical Interpretation

CHAPTER THREE

A (Complex) Simple Thread to Follow

How does God's love abide in anyone who has the
world's goods and sees a brother or sister in need and
yet refuses to help?

—1 John 3:17

One day I was looking around inside my Bible when I came
across this thread. The longer I looked at it, the longer it grew.
In fact, this thread stretched all the way from Exodus to 1
John. It began in Exodus 22, which says, "If you lend money
to the poor, you shall not charge them interest." And from
there, the thread wound its way over to Leviticus 19: "When
you reap the harvest of your land, you shall not reap to the
edges of your field . . . you shall leave the edges for the poor."
It surfaced again in Deuteronomy 15: "Do not be hard-
hearted or tight-fisted toward your needy neighbor . . . open
your hand to the poor." The thread appeared briefly in
Proverbs 17, "Those who mock the poor insult the Lord," and
I got a good look at it in Isaiah 58, "Share your bread with the
hungry and bring the homeless poor into your house. When
you see the naked clothe them." It then grew very dark in

Amos: Thus says the Lord, "I know how great are your sins, you who push aside the needy."

The thread must be about as strong as it is long, because it didn't break between the two testaments. It was still going in Matthew 19, where Jesus said, "Go, sell your possessions and give the money to the poor . . . then come follow me." And in Matthew 25, Jesus got the thread and Judgement Day all tangled up together when he said,

> Then the king will say to those on his right hand, Come you that are blessed by my Father, inherit the kingdom prepared for you from the foundation of the world; for I was hungry and you gave me food. I was thirsty and you gave me drink. I was a stranger and you welcomed me. I was naked and you gave me clothing. I was sick and you took care of me. I was in prison and you visited me.

The thread reappeared in Luke 4, where Jesus said, "The Spirit of the Lord is upon me, because he has anointed me to bring good news to the poor"; in Luke 6, when Jesus said, "Give to everyone who begs from you"; and in Luke 14, where Jesus said, "When you give a luncheon or a dinner, do not invite your friends or relatives or rich neighbors, but invite the poor, the crippled, the lame, the blind." The thread emerged in Acts 4:

> Now the whole group of those who believed were of one heart and soul, and no one claimed private ownership of any possessions, but everything they owned was held in common. . . . There was not a needy person among them, because as many as owned lands or houses sold them and brought the proceeds of the sale, and it was distributed to any who had need.

It peeked through in James 2: "If a brother or sister is naked and lacks daily food, and one of you says to them, 'Go in peace. Keep warm and eat your fill' and yet you do not supply their bodily needs, what good is that?" And finally the thread tied its crowning knot in 1 John: "How does God's love abide in anyone who has this world's goods and sees a brother or sister in need and yet refuses to help them?"

That's about it. That's the long and winding thread that I found inside my Bible: A simple thread of passionate concern for the poor; a thread of verses that call for those with resources to use them to lift and relieve the lives of those who struggle. That's it, plain and simple.

But that's where the simplicity ends and the complexity begins. Knowing what to do with that simple thread can be awfully complicated. Those simple verses that call us to respond to those who struggle pose hard questions. For example, since one cannot respond to every need, how does one choose which needs to meet? Then, there's the whole issue of what kind of help really helps, as opposed to help that only creates and perpetuates dependency. And the complexity doesn't end there. What about the possibility that some of our acts of mercy are just efforts at assuaging our guilt for living so easily in a world full of such pain and poverty? What about that? And anyway, isn't some of this "compassion for the poor" just do-gooderism, just more "social gospel" liberalism? What about that?

That the thread of passionate concern for the poor runs all through the Bible is inarguably clear. But that is where the clarity ends and the complexity begins. So what do we do? We must begin with the fact that the thread is there, and that no claim of taking the Bible seriously can fail to embrace God's call for God's people to care for and respond to the poor, the weak, the needy, and the vulnerable. Starting there, this is how we can live into the complexities. First of all, we can come to terms with the fact that if we wait until we can help everybody before we help anybody, then we are destined to help nobody.

So we must help somebody. We must defend somebody. We must feed somebody.

As for the complexity of knowing when help is truly helpful and when it merely perpetuates dependency . . . well, that's a hard one. I will have to leave the fine points of that endless complexity to brighter minds than mine. I don't know the answer to that one, but I do know what that thread that runs through the Bible says. We must try to be wise and discerning about how we help, but our bottom line is a thread, a thread of Bible verses that compel us to care about and respond to those in need. But do we do all of that so we can feel better about ourselves? I don't think so. I think we do it because the love of God is in us, and because we take the Bible seriously. And as for wondering if helping others is a sort of bleeding-heart-liberal-social-gospel kind of thing, all I know to do with that is to go back to the Bible. I mean, the Bible has this thread running through it, and in my own experience, the more conservative I become about the Bible's words, the more liberal I become about responding to people's needs.

In his book, *And Also With You,* Will Campbell recalls the January day in 1974 when Mississippi's Episcopal leaders met at St. Andrew's Cathedral in Jackson to elect a new bishop. Prominent among the names on the ballot was Duncan Gray Jr., who had spoken with great clarity and courage on the gospel side of the struggle for civil rights. Campbell writes that Duncan Gray's prophetic stand on the issues of the day had left many of his colleagues reluctant to elect him to the office of Bishop because they feared that he was too liberal. Campbell observed that their fears were misplaced. Duncan Gray was not too liberal for them; to the contrary, he was too conservative for them. It was his commitment to conserving the central truth of Scripture that compelled him to take such "liberal" social stands on controversial issues. It was Gray's unyielding conservatism about the Bible and the Prayer Book that had made him such a radical liberal in the eyes of some of his colleagues.[1]

Will Campbell's reflection on the work of Duncan Gray puts a human face on the fact that the more "conservative" one becomes about the Bible, the more "liberal" one will sometimes seem, as popular culture measures "conservatism" and "liberalism." The more committed one is to conserving what the Bible really says, the more liberal one becomes concerning care for the poor. The more conservative one becomes about the Bible, the more one's heart bleeds.

There is plenty of complexity here. To deny the complexity would be not to take seriously the world in which we live. But if we retreat into the complexity and hide behind it and close our eyes to the poor, then we will find ourselves in the awkward position of having to steer clear of the Bible, because there is this thread that runs through the Bible. The last time I saw it, it said, "If you, having this world's goods, see your brother or sister in need and refuse to help, then how can you say that the love of God is in you?" The complex questions around the edges of that thread can tie us in knots, but the simple truth at the center of it can bind us to the poor.

So be careful the next time you go looking around inside a Bible. If you read the Bible and speak the truth about what you find there, you might get tangled up in this long thread and end up looking like some kind of bleeding heart conservative.

Amen.

* * * * *

... Whereso'er you are,
That bide the pelting of this pitiless storm,
How shall your houseless heads and unfed
sides,
Your looped and windowed raggedness, defend
you
From seasons such as these. Oh, I have taken
Too little care of this!

—*Lear, in Shakespeare's* King Lear

NOTE

[1] Will Campbell, *And Also With You* (Franklin: Providence House Publishers, 1997), 203.

CHAPTER FOUR

Whatever We Ask?

"The Father will give you whatever you ask in my name."
—*John 15:16*

We receive from God whatever we ask, because we obey
God's commandments and do what pleases God.
—*1 John 3:22*

"We receive from God whatever we ask." "Ask for whatever you wish, and it will be done for you." "The Father will give you whatever you ask in my name." Sometimes I wonder how those words sound on other ears. In mine, they sound hopeful and beautiful. But some place deeper than my ears, those words that sound so beautiful feel so bewildering because I can remember times when I have asked for good things, in the right spirit, with pure motives, and sometimes those prayers have brought the result for which I prayed and sometimes they haven't. I imagine that I am not alone in that experience. There isn't a believer who prays who hasn't had that same experience. You pray your hardest and believe your deepest, and sometimes things turn out the way you prayed, and sometimes they don't. This wouldn't be quite so bewildering if it weren't for all those Bible verses that sound almost like airtight guarantees that if we pray for the right things in the right way we will always receive *whatever we ask.*

So, what do we do? How do we bridge the gap between what we read in Scripture and what we experience in life? Sometimes we just blame ourselves. "If I had prayed harder or longer, God would have healed her. If I had gotten more people to join with me in prayer, God would have protected him." That is popular religious language. It sees prayer as a transaction; if I offer God *enough* (enough intensity, enough time, enough voices), I can persuade God to do a wonderful thing that God would not otherwise have done out of God's own goodness. If I offer God the proper currency of sufficient faith or adequate intensity, then, in exchange, God will come around and do what I want. But can that be a truthful way to think of God? Think about what that view of prayer says about God. It says that God has to be worn down by our persistence before God can be persuaded to do our will. (Remember, the "persistence parables" in Luke 11 and 18 are parables of contrast, not comparison. They show us the way God is by showing us the way God isn't.)

If we are going to have a doctrine of prayer, it needs to be a doctrine worthy of our doctrine of God. Good theology always begins with God. We don't start by figuring out what we believe about prayer and then bending what we believe about God to fit our doctrine of prayer. Rather, we start by settling what we believe about God. We start with God—"In the beginning God." Then, having settled what we believe about God, we read all those Bible verses about prayer, and we are honest about our own undeniable experiences with prayer, and then we arrive at a doctrine of prayer that is worthy of the best that we know of God.

Starting with God and developing a view of prayer worthy of my best understanding of who God is has brought me to a place in life where I see prayer not as a transaction, but as a confession; a perpetual confession of hopes and desires and yearnings for God to do that which is best; a perpetual stream of confession that I could not stop even if I tried. That is a view of prayer that I found while stumbling around in a canyon. The canyon exists between those "whatever you ask" Bible verses and the undeniable reality of my own experience with prayer. We need an honest, real, true-to-God view of prayer. Our view of prayer cannot be determined by popular religious culture's simplistic, bumper-sticker approach to life's great mysteries.

We cannot even have a view of prayer determined by an isolated verse of Scripture here and there, because the Bible does not speak with one carefully homogenized, smooth, seamless voice about prayer. Rather, we have to read the whole Bible—all those "whatever you ask" verses and all those other verses from Job and the Psalms and Jeremiah that record other voices crying out, "My God, My God, why have you forsaken me? Why don't you hear me? Why don't you answer me?" Those Bible verses are there, too. So we read the whole Bible and speak the truth about what we discover. We look at our whole life, and tell the truth about what we have experienced. We make what we believe about God the touchstone and benchmark for everything else, and then—only then—are we ready to decide what we believe about the great, beautiful, bewildering, glorious mystery of prayer.

But what about all those "whatever you ask" verses, with their various conditions and contingencies for success or failure? Does prayer ever actually alter outcomes? Does our praying ever actually cause things to turn out differently than they would have if we had not prayed? My answer to that mystery—my most honest, unvarnished answer—is "Yes."

The reason I say "Yes" is because I believe that the great heart of God that is somehow broken by our pain is also somehow moved by our praying. Because I believe that about God, I believe that our praying does somehow alter outcomes. But why not always? Why not in every case? That is the great mystery. That is the question that carves a canyon between the "whatever we ask" Bible verses and the darkest, hardest struggles of our lives. The mystery is there, and it must be honored for the mystery that it is. That is why I believe that it is enough to say, "The great heart of God that is somehow broken by our pain is also somehow moved by our praying." To say much more than that may be to say too much. I'll take pure mystery over poor theology any day, and hurling too many clichés at this great mystery lands us in poor theology pretty quickly.

And, anyway, it's very biblical to let the mystery of prayer be as bewildering as it really is. Remember what Paul said in Romans 8:26, "We do not know how to pray." But that's all right because of what Paul says in Romans 8:27, "But God knows how to hear." When it comes to prayer, we don't know how to pray, but God knows how to hear. If we believe the right things about God, then that's all we need to know about prayer to keep us praying for as long as we live.

Plus, that puts what we believe about prayer back on what we believe about God, which is where it belongs anyway.

Amen.

* * * * *

> When I pray, coincidences happen. When I don't pray, they don't.
>
> —*William Temple, Archbishop of Canterbury*

CHAPTER FIVE

How Much Faith Is Enough?

Immediately he made the disciples get into the boat and go on ahead to the other side, while he dismissed the crowds. And after he had dismissed the crowds, he went up the mountain by himself to pray. When evening came, he was there alone, but by this time the boat, battered by the waves, was far from the land, for the wind was against them. And early in the morning he came walking toward them on the sea.

But when the disciples saw him walking on the sea, they were terrified, saying, "It is a ghost!" And they cried out in fear.

But immediately Jesus spoke to them and said, "Take heart, it is I; do not be afraid."

Peter answered him, "Lord, if it is you, command me to come to you on the water." He said, "Come." So Peter got out of the boat, started walking on the water, and came toward Jesus. But when he noticed the strong wind, he became frightened, and beginning to sink, he cried out, "Lord save me!" Jesus immediately reached out his hand and caught him, saying to him, "You of little faith, why did you doubt?" When they got into the boat,

> the wind ceased. And those in the boat worshiped him,
> saying, "Truly you are the Son of God."
>
> —*Matthew 14:22-32*

Were it not for the Gospel of Matthew, we would never have known about Peter's brief walk on the wild side of a rough sea. We cannot know Matthew's original purposes for including the stormy episode, but we do know that Matthew's story of Peter's faith and fear became a mirror in which believers have been able to see themselves all across the centuries. The convergence of faith and fear constitutes a great struggle for many Christians. Why do believers have their doubts? For that matter, where do believers get their faith? Is faith a gift? Or is it a choice? Is faith a purely individual matter between a person and God? Or is faith what we find in a community of believers and share with a family of faith? And while we're on the subject, how much faith is enough? If you have too little, how do you get more?

Because I believe that those questions are so central to so many lives, I decided I had to reread all four Gospels with a special focus on those places where Jesus talks about faith and believing. I marked in purple every spot where the word "faith" comes up. That left me with eleven purple marks in Matthew, nine in Mark and thirteen in Luke. Many of those instances are, of course, duplicate verses from one gospel to another. Most of them are occasions when Jesus reprimands his followers for having so little faith or praises a stranger for having so much.

And then there is John's Gospel, where I never even uncapped my purple pen. Not one time does the noun "faith" show up in John's gospel. What we have in John, instead of the noun "faith," is the verb "believe." Forty times in John's Gospel we come across the idea of "believing." In John, unlike Matthew, Mark, and Luke, there isn't a single place that suggests there are "amounts of faith" or "levels of believing." There is no suggestion that you can "believe a lot" or "believe a little." You either believe that Jesus is the one sent from God or you don't. And here's something really fascinating: In John's Gospel, believing that Jesus is the one sent from God is the way to eternal life, but it is never the prerequisite for a miracle. In Matthew, Mark, and Luke, it's just the opposite. Faith is frequently the prerequisite for a miracle, but eternal life is tied not to faith, but to decisive action: Deny yourself, take up the cross, follow me.

It took me about ten hours to read all four Gospels through, word for word. You ought to try it sometime, focusing especially on the places where faith comes up. It is an overwhelming experience that leaves you knowing that there are no simple answers to the hardest questions we can ponder about faith. (Show me someone who can offer a smooth, seamless synopsis of what the Bible says about faith, and I'll show you someone who hasn't been reading the Bible!)

In the Gospels, people seem either to have faith or not have faith, which raises the question, "Is faith a gift from God?" In the same sense that some are gifted to make music or write poems or guide organizations, are some simply gifted to believe? Do some people come into this world just wired-up for easy believing, while others come wired-up for perpetual questioning that makes believing more difficult? Is that it? Is faith a gift that one either does or does not have? And if it is a gift and I don't have it, how can I get it? That's the real question. Of course, maybe faith isn't a gift. Maybe faith is a choice. Perhaps faith is not so much a gift God gives us as it is a way of life we choose. Whether faith is gift or choice or both, this much is certain: For some, believing comes easily. For others, it feels like breaking rocks under the blazing sun. This difference doesn't make the easy believer "more spiritual" than the struggling seeker. It's just a fact about life, faith, and the life of faith.

Of course, beyond the question of whether an individual's faith is a gift or a choice is the question of whether faith belongs to an individual at all. Peter's faith, you will recall, did best in the boat. His faith was only revealed to be too light to float when he left the community to go freelancing on his own. Barbara Brown Taylor says that if Peter had had more faith, he would have stayed in the boat with the others and waited on Jesus.[1] After all, Jesus had already identified himself. But Peter had to be sure, so he said, "If it's really you, command me to walk on water, too." There was no reason for Peter to leave the boat and walk on water. His freelancing was, as Taylor points out, more an act of doubt than an act of faith. He should have stayed in the boat with the other believers.

Maybe faith is not nearly as individual as we make it out to be. Maybe we put too much pressure on our own faith. Maybe we do best when we see ourselves as contributors to, recipients of, and dependents on the faith of the community of believers. Do not try this at home. In the family of faith, we bear one another's burdens of sorrow and sickness, and we can also bear the burden of one another's doubt and disbelief. (Remember the miracle of the man lowered through the roof and healed by Jesus. For all we know, he may have had no faith. The Scripture says that Jesus saw *the faith of his friends.*)

Faith as gift . . . faith as choice . . . faith as the shared believing of gathered believers. There are hints and clues of all these definitions in the Gospels. And the haunting question also loiters in the shadows, "How much faith is enough?" "If I had more faith, I know God would have healed her." "If we'll just have enough faith, he'll be all right." That language has long held a large place in the lives of many sincere believers. If you read Matthew, Mark, and Luke, you can see why. When miracles don't come, there is sometimes the reprimand, "O, you of little faith." The assumption we have derived from these words is that having more faith equals seeing more miracles. But, of course, it isn't that simple, because throughout the gospel of John, the miracles are the producers of belief, not the products of believing. And anyway, once we start basing what God does on how much faith we have, we have shifted our trust from God and put our trust in our own capacity to believe. In other words, our faith is now in our faith, not in God. Thus, we, not God, are in control. We are at the center of the universe, and all God's initiative is on hold, waiting to see how much we believe. Can that be true?

It's a complex picture frequently framed by those familiar verses, "If you had faith the size of a mustard seed, you could say to this mountain, 'Move,' and it would." I have had that much faith before in the face of mountains—mountains, I am here to report, that have not always moved. But, to be perfectly honest, when the mountains have not moved, my mustard seed of faith has not diminished one bit. I no longer have it in me to be disillusioned with God or disenchanted by mountains of sorrow or sickness or trouble that stay put. It's not because I have so much faith. It has less to do with faith in God than it has to do with love for God. In 1 Corinthians 13, the Bible says, "Love believes all things." This is the glorious, wide-eyed naiveté of love: Love believes all things. When you come to that place in life where you love God unconditionally, demanding nothing in return, then it sets you free to keep believing, even when the mountains don't move. When you love God unconditionally, you can pray with faith and live believing in the face of a thousand disappointments, and you still know that God is yet at work doing wonderful things. Some theologians call it "the second naiveté." I call it loving God unconditionally with the love that believes all things. That is the kind of love for God that looks like faith in God.

Such faith is enough faith to keep us on our feet in life's worst storms, if we'll just remember to stay in the boat with our sisters and brothers and leave the fancy footwork to Jesus.

Amen.

* * * * *

How brittle are the piers
On which our faith doth tread –
No bridge below doth totter so,
Yet none hath such a crowd.

It is as old as God –
Indeed, 'twas built by Him
He sent His son to test the plank,
And he pronounced it firm.

—*Emily Dickinson*

NOTE

[1] Barbara Brown Taylor, *Bread of Angels* (Boston: Cowley Publications, 1997), 122.

24

CHAPTER SIX

When the Questions Are Deeper than the Sea

On that day, when evening had come, he said to them, "Let us go across to the other side." And leaving the crowd behind, they took him with them in the boat, just as he was. Other boats were with him. A great windstorm arose, and the waves beat into the boat, so that the boat was already being swamped. But he was in the stern, asleep on the cushion; and they woke him up and said to him, "Teacher, do you not care that we are perishing?"

He woke up and rebuked the wind, and said to the sea, "Peace! Be still!" Then the wind ceased, and there was a dead calm. He said to them, "Why are you afraid? Have you still no faith?"

And they were filled with great awe and said to one another, "Who then is this, that even the wind and the sea obey him?"

—*Mark 4:35-41*

The wind howls, the waves crash, the boat begins to sink, the disciples are perishing, and Jesus is—yes, that's right—dozing! While the disciples are drowning, Jesus is dreaming. While they snorkel, he snores. When they finally rouse him, it is with a question rougher than the water: "Wake up," they say. "Do you not care that we are going under?"

If their words seem a bit harsh, we must remember that what the disciples in the storm asked Jesus is not unlike what other souls in other storms have been asking God for a long, long time. Take Moses, for example, in the book of Numbers, crying out to God, "Why have you treated me so badly? Why have you placed this awful burden on me?" In Judges 6, Gideon cries out, "If the Lord is with us, why have such bad things happened to us? And where are the Lord's wonderful deeds that our ancestors were always telling us about?" Job calls out to God, "Why have you made me your target? Why do you hide your face from me?" The writer in Psalm 10 laments, "Why, O Lord, do you stand far off? Why do you hide yourself in times of trouble?" And in Psalm 13, "How long, O Lord? Will you forget me forever? How long will you hide your face from me? How long must I bear pain in my soul and have sorrow in my heart? Answer me, O Lord!" And in Psalm 22, "My God, my God, why have you forsaken me? Why are you so far from helping me?" And in Psalm 77, "Has God forgotten to be gracious? Are God's promises over? Will the Lord spurn us forever?" Then the prophet Jeremiah hurls his piercing questions to God: "Why is my pain unceasing and my wound incurable? Why can't I be healed?" Habakkuk takes up the cry when he asks, "O Lord, how long shall I cry for help and you will not listen?" Those are hard questions, asked of God by people staggering through storms, people who cannot find God or hear God in the midst of their awful turmoil.

It might be helpful for us to remember that one thing all those people had in common was the depth of their relationship to God. I grew up in a world where people would often say, in the face of tragedy or sorrow, "Well, we mustn't question God. No, no. We can't question God." Where in the world did we get that notion? The phrase, "We mustn't question God" ought to be forever banished from the vocabulary of God's people. Read the Bible. Who were those people questioning God? Bad people? Weak people? Faithless people? I don't think so. Moses, Gideon, Job, Jeremiah, Habakkuk, the Psalmist. These are among the brightest and best children of God. Not to mention Jesus, dying on the cross. Jesus could have picked anything from his Jewish storehouse to quote on the cross. But what he chose was one of those questions for God: "My God, my God, why have you forsaken me?" (Ps 22:1).

Those kinds of questions emerge from the deepest corners of the darkest struggles people face. The people who ask those kinds of questions tend to be the people closest to God. If you don't really believe, you don't ask those kinds of questions. Those hard questions for God are not symptoms of disbelief in God. They are signs of a living faith that expects God's presence to make a difference. Unless you truly expect God to be present, you don't inquire so passionately into God's apparent absence. You have to expect God to be active to ask, "Why aren't you doing more? Why don't you intervene more powerfully?" Those are the questions of real believers with real expectations, believers bewildered by God's apparent silence, absence, and inactivity.

Those are perfectly reasonable questions. If God is so loving and caring and compassionate, and if God is so powerful and able and aware, then times of trial certainly raise the question: "If God cares and if God can, then why?" "Lord, do you not care that we are perishing?" "If you care and if you can, why don't you just fix things and deliver us from our longest, darkest, worst struggles?" One wise and honest struggler once said, "'Why' is the question-mark that is twisted like a fish-hook in the heart."[1] And so it is. Nicholas Wolterstorff, writing about his son's tragic death, said, "I cannot make it all fit together by saying, 'God did it,' but neither can I make it all fit together by saying there was nothing God could do about it. I cannot fit it all together. I can only . . . endure."[2]

Wolterstorff was right. In the face of life's worst tragedies and darkest struggles, we cannot make it all fit together. It seems best that, in the face of life's deepest mysteries, we should let the questions stand unanswered, because most of the answers are poor, and a deep question beats a shallow answer any day. Better to struggle with deep questions that forever go unanswered than to settle for shallow answers that forever go unquestioned.

Amen.

* * * * *

To live without the answer is precarious.
It's hard to keep one's footing.

—*Nicholas Wolterstorff*
Lament for a Son

NOTES

[1] Peter DeVries, *The Blood of the Lamb* (Boston: Little, Brown and Co., 1969), 243.

[2] Nicholas Wolterstorff, *Lament for a Son* (Grand Rapids: Eerdmans, 1985), 67.

CHAPTER SEVEN

On Simply Falling Silent

Then Job answered the Lord: "I know that you can do
all things,
and that no purpose of yours can be thwarted.
'Who is this that hides counsel without knowledge?
Therefore I have uttered what I did not understand,
things too wonderful for me, which I did not know.
'Hear, and I will speak;
I will question you, and you declare to me.
I had heard of you by the hearing of the ear,
but now my eye sees you;
therefore I despise myself,
and repent in dust and ashes."

After the Lord had spoken these words to Job, the Lord
said to Eliphaz the Temanite: "My wrath is kindled
against you and against your two friends; for you have not
spoken of me what is right, as my servant Job has. Now
therefore take seven bulls and seven rams, and go to my
servant Job, and offer up for yourselves a burnt offering;
and my servant Job shall pray for you, for I will accept
his prayer not to deal with you according to your folly;

for you have not spoken of me what is right, as my servant Job has done." So Eliphaz the Temanite and Bildad
the Shuhite and Zophar the Naamathite went and did
what the Lord had told them; and the Lord accepted Job's
prayer.

And the Lord restored the fortunes of Job when he
had prayed for his friends; and the Lord gave Job twice as
much as he had before. Then there came to him all his
brothers and sisters and all who had known him before,
and they ate bread with him in his house; they showed
him sympathy and comforted him for all the evil that the
Lord had brought upon him; and each of them gave him
a piece of money and a gold ring. The Lord blessed the
latter days of Job more than his beginning.

—Job 42:1-12

One of the Episcopal church's most widely quoted preachers is
an extraordinary minister and teacher named Barbara Brown
Taylor. In one of her books, Reverend Taylor offers this obser-
vation about Job: "You can read about Moses splitting the Red
Sea, or Deborah routing the Canaanites, and never once think
about your own life, but the minute Job climbs up on his
dung-heap and starts cursing the day he was born, it is hard
not to empathize."[1] Taylor is right. We may not be able to
relate to Noah floating his zoo or to David guarding his flock,
but when we hear Job asking his questions, we understand.
When Job wonders why God sometimes seems so silent and
absent in the dark places and the terrible struggles, we relate.
When Job wishes God would protect and spare the innocent
and good from tragedy and terror, we connect. When Job cries
out for some honest resolution to the mystery of seemingly
senseless human suffering, we agree. Sooner or later, somewhere along the way, Job's story will likely become our story.

The last chapter of Job's story is a chapter full of lessons
for us to learn from Job's two sets of friends, lessons about

what to do and not to do in the face of enormous tragedy and devastating loss. From Job's first set of friends—Eliphaz, Bildad, and Zophar—there are lessons for us to learn about what not to do in the face of someone else's sorrow. We meet Eliphaz, Bildad, and Zophar early in the book of Job. Job's vast business enterprise has been wiped out by a series of catastrophes. His ten children have all perished in a single disaster. Finally, his healthy body has been afflicted with a dreadful disease that makes his life miserable every day. The best person anyone has ever known is now suffering the worst trouble anyone has ever seen. When Eliphaz, Bildad, and Zophar hear of Job's awful grief, they come to visit him. At first, they simply fall silent and sit quietly with Job. (So far, so good.) But before long, Job's friends begin to offer explanations for Job's dreadful agonies. They repeat to Job what they have always heard, which is that God protects and prospers the truly righteous. Thus, given the incredible magnitude of Job's suffering, they can only conclude that Job is not as innocent as everyone always assumed. But Job is unmoved, because Job knows that he has done nothing to merit this kind of suffering.

Job's friends want him to acquiesce to the familiar answers of their religious tradition and conventional wisdom. Job refuses to accept their explanations, however, because his own undeniable experience does not support what they tell him to believe. Rather than settling for the answers of others, he raises his own questions and complaints. In chapter 7, Job says, "I will not restrain my mouth. I will speak in the anguish of my spirit and I will complain in the bitterness of my soul. Why have you made me your target, God? Why have I become a burden to you?" In Job 10, he laments, "Why do you contend against me? Does it seem good to you to oppress and despise the work of your hands? . . . You know that I am not guilty. Leave me alone, God, that I might find a little comfort." But

Job's friends cannot bear to hear him cry out to God with such unadorned honesty in such unorthodox words. So they rebuke him. In chapter 11, one of them says, "Should such talk as this go unanswered? You are mocking God; shall no one shame you? You say you are clean in God's sight, but the truth is, the agony God has sent you is less than your guilt deserves."

Eliphaz, Bildad, and Zophar ardently defend God against Job's heresy and rage. They are God's bodyguards. One would expect God to be grateful for their support. But instead, what we find is the exact opposite. In the passage from the last chapter of Job, God says to Eliphaz, "My anger is kindled against you and Bildad and Zophar; for you have not spoken of me what is right as my servant Job has." God's apologists have said too much. They have spoken with too much certainty in the face of too much mystery. God actually seems to favor Job's messy, angry, unsettling questions over their neat, seamless, settled explanations.

From Job's talkative friends Eliphaz, Bildad, and Zophar, there are lessons for us to learn concerning what not to do in the face of life's worst tragedies and greatest sorrows. What we must not do is jump in with too many glib religious clichés and simplistic theological explanations. We mean well, of course. Like Eliphaz, Bildad, and Zophar, we intend only the best. But as soon as we start saying things such as, "Well, God makes no mistakes," or "God won't put any more on us than we can bear," then we imply that God sent the tragedy. In our effort to defend God, we implicate God. One of my most memorable examples of such efforts to "defend God" in the face of tragedy comes from William Sloane Coffin's sermon, "Alex's Death," the first sermon Dr. Coffin preached after his twenty-two-year-old son, Alex, died in a tragic accident. Coffin says in his sermon that a visitor who came to his home after Alex's death assigned the tragedy to "the will of God," and then said, "I just don't understand God's will." Coffin said he replied to the person, "I'll say you don't understand God's will! God's will did not cause Alex's death. When will otherwise intelligent people ever get it through their heads that God doesn't go around with a hand on steering wheels and a finger on triggers!"[2] William Sloane Coffin's well-intentioned comforter, in a sincere effort to offer a religious word, over-spoke. We have to be careful, or we will say too much, and sometimes what we say is unworthy of the God we intend to defend. (Just ask Eliphaz, Bildad, and Zophar!)

But those three friends are not our only teachers in the classroom of Job 42. From Eliphaz, Bildad, and Zophar we learn a lesson about what *not* to do in the face of enormous tragedy and devastating loss. But from another group of Job's friends, an unnamed group of caregivers, we learn what to do. The second set of friends appears in Job 42:11, which says, "Then came to Job all who had known him, and they ate bread with Job, they showed him sympathy and comforted him . . . and each of them gave Job a piece of money and a gold ring." This second set of friends, these anonymous caregivers, didn't bring explanations; they brought food. They didn't preach to Job; they ate with Job. They didn't give theories; they gave money. From these friends, we learn a better lesson, a lesson about what to do: Show up. Bring food. Write notes. Send flowers. Offer help. Hug. Weep. Pray. Listen. And beyond that . . . well, beyond that the best we can do is to stare into the mystery that lies beyond our understanding and simply fall silent, lest, like Job's other friends, we say more than we know.

Amen.

* * * * *

Don't cry, dear Mary. Let us do that for you, because you are too tired now. We don't know how dark it is, but if you are at sea, perhaps when we say that we are there, you won't be as afraid. The waves are very big, but every one that covers you, covers us, too. Dear Mary, you can't see us, but we are close at your side. May we comfort you?

—*Emily Dickinson, in a letter to a friend*

NOTES

[1] Barbara Brown Taylor, *Home By Another Way* (Boston: Cowley Publications, 1997), 162.

[2] *A Chorus of Witnesses*, eds. Thomas G. Long and Cornelius Platinga Jr. (Grand Rapids: Wm. B. Eerdmans, 1994), 264.

CHAPTER EIGHT

Joseph's Choice

Then Joseph could no longer control himself before all those who stood by him and he cried out, "Send everyone away from me." So no one stayed with him when Joseph made himself known to his brothers. And he wept so loudly that the Egyptians heard it, and the household of Pharaoh heard it. Joseph said to his brothers, "I am Joseph. Is my father still alive?" But his brothers could not answer him, so dismayed were they at his presence.

Then Joseph said to his brothers, "Come closer to me." And they came closer. He said, "I am your brother Joseph, whom you sold into Egypt. And now do not be distressed, or angry with yourselves, because you sold me here; for God sent me before you to preserve life. For the famine has been in the land these two years; and there are five more years in which there will be neither plowing nor harvest. God sent me before you to preserve for you a remnant on earth, and to keep alive for you many survivors. So it was not you who sent me here, but God; he has made me a father to Pharaoh, and lord of all his house and ruler over all the land of Egypt. Hurry up and go up to my father and say to him, 'Thus says your son Joseph, God has made me lord of all Egypt; come down to me, do not delay. You shall settle in the land of Goshen, and you shall be near me, you and your children and your children's children, a well as your flocks, your herds, and all that you have. I will provide for you there—since there are five more years of famine to come—so that you and your household, and all that you have, will not come to poverty. And now your eyes and the eyes of my brother Benjamin see that it is my own mouth that speaks to you. You must tell my father how greatly I am honored in Egypt, and all that you have seen. Hurry and bring my father down here." Then he fell upon his brother Benjamin's neck and wept, while Benjamin wept upon his neck. And he kissed all his brothers and wept upon them; and after that his brothers talked to him.

—*Genesis 45:1-15*

He knows that they are them, but they don't know that he is him. Years ago, they threw him in a pit and sold him into slavery. Now, he is the bread marshall of Egypt, and they have come seeking food in a time of famine. The one they once treated so shabbily now runs the bakery. The one they once wronged so fiercely now holds their destiny in his hands. And to make matters worse, he knows that they are them, but they don't know that he is him. That is, until the dramatic moment when Joseph can no longer bear to continue the charade.

Talk about high drama! What a moment! The Bible says Joseph's brothers were so dismayed they couldn't speak. I bet. The last time they saw Joseph to recognize him, he was being carted off to a life of bondage into which they, his own brothers, had sold him. And now, he's on the throne and they're on the spot. He's sitting in the high-chair and they're squirming on the hot-seat. What will Joseph do? This is his chance for revenge. They've got it coming. Only, it never comes. Joseph makes a different choice. Joseph could have chosen bitterness and revenge.

Instead he chose kindness and mercy. These brothers of his had done him wrong. They had cast him away, placed him in danger, sent him into slavery, and even trumped up evidence of his death to fool their father into thinking that Joseph had been killed by a wild beast. And yet, when he finally had them under his thumb, he wrapped them in his arms.

To borrow a phrase from Ferrol Sams, this story has "more layers than a hen-yard."[1] It is a story of parental favoritism, sibling rivalry, and family division. It is a story about dreams and their interpretation, about the pressures of temptation, and about choices between vengeance and reconciliation. All of that and more is woven into the ancient drama of Joseph's story, which makes the Joseph story in Genesis a parable of real life in the real world, here and now for you and me. There are many lessons for life that span the space between Joseph's world and ours, one of which concerns the clear vision that only comes with the passage of time.

We should probably remember that when Joseph said to his brothers, "It was not you who sent me here, but God," that was Joseph's perspective many years after the fact. Back when he was in the middle of the trouble, all he saw was trouble. At the time, he could not see the hand of God at work in the terrible ordeal into which he had been hurled by his brutal brothers. Joseph had to live beyond the events themselves, get further down the road, and look back on his terrible troubles in order to make sense of them. It may be a well-worn cliché, but it is nonetheless true that "Life can only be lived forward and understood backward," or, to put it another way, "The will of God is much easier to see in retrospect than it is in prospect." Joseph had gotten twenty years down the road from his awful struggle in the pit and the prison. The further he got from his deepest hurts and worst wounds, the better he could see how God, wonder of wonders, had used his troubles to shape his life for good.

Such is the way life almost always works. We usually cannot see all that is happening in any present moment. Some time has to pass. Then, when we get far enough away from the crisis, the disappointment, the hurt, or the tragedy, we can sometimes begin to discern more clearly from a distance what we could not see up close. (Not always, of course. Some things will never make an ounce of sense. Some things will always remain senseless and pointless and unredeemable as far as we can see . . . but not many.) Most of the time, that old gospel song proves true: "Farther along we'll know more about it."[2] That was certainly true for Joseph. He lived long enough to be able to say of that terrible time in his life, "You meant what you did to harm me, but God turned your bad deed to good. You intended to send me to slavery, but God turned your evil intention to a wonderful surprise." That is not the way it looked when it happened. That is the way it looked from the distance of twenty years of time.

None of us wants to wait that long to decipher the mystery of life's worst wounds and deepest hurts. And most of the time, it doesn't take that much time. But it always takes some time to get far enough away from a terrible loss or a dark betrayal or a painful struggle to be able to see what formerly unimaginable goodness has emerged as the rest of life has unfolded.

I wonder if we try to start understanding too soon, if we expect to make too much sense of too much mystery in too little time. I wonder if sometimes we expect to be able to forgive too soon. Joseph is a great model of forgiveness, but Joseph's life had turned out pretty rosy. When Joseph said to his brothers, "You meant to do me harm, but God turned your evil intention to good," Joseph was speaking from the vantage point of twenty-something years. Perhaps he could have said the same thing sooner, but we will never know. What we do know is that in a world where people do terrible things to one another, in a world where all of us are sinners, a world where deep hurts are borne and awful wounds are worn; forgiveness does not always happen in a day. Honest forgiveness that deals truthfully with sin and refuses the dishonesty of cheap grace and repressed anger may take a while. How can it not take time? In a letter to a friend, C. S. Lewis once wrote, "Last week, while at prayer, I suddenly discovered that I had really forgiven someone I had been trying to forgive for over thirty years. For thirty years I had been praying that I might, and trying to forgive him." Commenting on C. S. Lewis' words, in his book *Embodying Forgiveness*, Gregory Jones says, "Thirty years might seem an extraordinarily long time to some, realistic to others, and to yet others—particularly those who have unjustly suffered something of great magnitude—it might seem brief."[3]

It was a long time after his brothers did him wrong before Joseph could say, "What you did with evil intention, God turned to something good." Joseph could only see that from a distance. Joseph chose to forgive a great wound, but Joseph's choice came after life had worked out well, many years later. We mustn't interpret that as an excuse, as a license to pet a grudge, nurse a wound, and let the sun set on our anger until it hardens into bitterness. That would be a sin against God's grace, against the example of Jesus, and against our own selves, because our bitterness, of course, finally destroys no one but us. We don't need to appeal to Joseph's twenty years or C. S. Lewis' thirty to let ourselves off the hook and give ourselves an excuse for bitterness. But maybe we do have to give ourselves time for forgiveness. While that time passes, we must live, act, and speak as though we are on the way to forgiveness. If we live, act, and speak as people on the way to bitterness, then that is probably where we will end up. If, on the other hand, we go ahead and begin living, acting, and speaking as though we expect someday to arrive at forgiveness, we'll eventually get there. And, in the meantime, perhaps we have to let the church forgive for us what we, all alone, cannot yet forgive. Maybe it not only doesn't happen all at once, maybe it also doesn't happen all alone. Do not try this at home. The capacity to make Joseph's beautiful choice comes not only with the passage of time but also with the support of people. Even then, it is a mighty and wonderful work of God, who has a long career of bringing unimaginable good from unspeakable pain.

Amen.

* * * * *

> The sad things that happened long ago will always remain part of who we are, just as the glad and gracious things will too, but instead of being a burden of guilt, recrimination and regret that make us constantly stumble as we go, even the saddest things can become, once we have made peace with them, a source of wisdom and strength for the journey that still lies ahead. It is through memory that we are able to reclaim much of our lives that we have long since written off, by finding that in everything that has happened to us over the years God was offering us possibilities of new life and healing which, though we may have missed them at the time, we can still choose and be brought to life by and healed by all these years later.
>
> —*Frederick Buechner*
> Telling Secrets

NOTES

[1] Ferrol Sams, endorsement for Will Campbell's *The Stem of Jesse* (Macon Ga: Mercer University Press, 1995).

[2] Copyright 1937 Stamps-Baxter Music (admin. by Benson Music Group, Inc.).

[3] L. Gregory Jones, *Embodying Forgiveness* (Grand Rapids: Wm. B. Eerdmans, 1995), 236.

CHAPTER NINE

Something Short of a Tragedy

Lord, you have been our dwelling place
    in all generations.
Before the mountains were brought forth,
        or ever you had formed the earth
            and the world,
        from everlasting to everlasting you are God.

You turn us back to dust,
    and say, "Turn back, you mortals."
For a thousand years in your sight
    are like yesterday when it is past,
    or like a watch in the night.
You sweep them away; they are like a dream,
    like grass that is renewed in the morning;
in the morning it flourishes and is renewed;
in the evening it fades and withers.
For we are consumed by your anger;
    by your wrath we are overwhelmed.
You have set our iniquities before you,
    our secret sins in the light of your countenance.
For all our days pass away under your wrath;

> our years come to an end like a sigh.
> The days of our life are seventy years,
>> or perhaps eighty, if we are strong;
> even then their span is only toil and trouble;
>> they are soon gone, and we fly away.
>
> Who considers the power of your anger?
>> Your wrath is as great as the fear that is due you.
> So teach us to count our days
>> that we may gain a wise heart.
>
> —*Psalm 90:1-12*

In a powerful corner of Anne Lamott's memoir *Traveling Mercies*, Lamott tells about the time she went shopping with her terminally ill friend, Pammy. They were in Macy's. Lamott was looking for a dress. She tried on one particular outfit, scrutinizing herself in the department store mirror, pondering how the dress fit and how it made her look and such, until Pammy said, "Anne, you don't have that kind of time."[1] From the vantage point of her wheelchair, with little of life left to live, Pammy had a special word of wisdom for those worried about too much that matters too little: "You don't have that kind of time." Pammy was right. Someday is going to be the last day. We must not act as though we have unlimited time, because we don't. "We don't have that kind of time."

No one anywhere has ever captured the passage of time and the limits of life more powerfully than did Thornton Wilder in the third act of his wonderful work, *Our Town*. Wilder's character Emily, upon returning from the place of the dead to relive her twelfth birthday, speaks the truth that we all need to face when she says, "I can't look at everything hard enough. . . . It goes so fast. We don't have time to look at one another." And then, when it's time for Emily to leave, she asks that unforgettable question, "Do any human beings ever realize life while they live it?—every, every minute?"[2]

Emily had learned how precious, passing, and fragile life really is. She had discovered the kind of time we have. The kind of time we have is the kind that passes, goes, flies, and slips away. The kind of time we have is the kind of time the psalmist measured in Psalm 90:

> All our days pass away, our years come to an end like a sigh. The days of our life are seventy years, or perhaps eighty if we are strong; even then their span is only toil and trouble. Our days are soon gone, and we fly away. So teach us to count our days, so that we may gain a wise heart.

The psalmist prays that God will "Teach us to count our days." To count our days means to recognize the fact that we do not have an infinite number of days, to realize that the time of our life is limited, to awaken to the fact that someday is going to be the last day. Facing the fact that someday is going to be the last day is not something to make us morbid or fatalistic or death-obsessed. In fact, the exact opposite is true. Living each day knowing that someday will be the last day is the only way to stay fully alive to the absolute sacredness of ordinary moments on routine days. One must first be awake to the fact that life is fleeting, passing, limited, and certain to end before one can really love and live any one day the way a single day of life deserves to be lived and loved.

In the book *Tuesdays with Morrie*, Morrie Schwartz said to his friend Mitch, "Everybody knows they're going to die, but nobody really believes it. If we did, we would do things differently. . . . Most of us walk around as if we're sleepwalking. We really don't experience our lives fully, because we're half-asleep. But when you realize you are going to die," Morrie concluded, "you see everything much differently. Once you learn how to die, you learn how to live."[3] That is the kind of wisdom for which the psalmist prayed, for the wise heart that belongs only to those who have learned to count their days.

We can become that wise. We can become as awake as the psalmist who said, "All our days pass away, our years come to an end like a sigh . . . Our days are soon gone, and we fly away . . . Teach us to count our days, so that we may gain a wise heart." Those who look at their own lives most wisely are those who have faced their own death most honestly. Life is slipping away. We don't have forever. And we won't get to try again. This is it. Everlasting life with God will be something else. But this limited, passing, fleeting life is the only one we will have here. The late humorist Lewis Grizzard was so right when he said, concerning our fragile, fleeting lives, "This ain't no dress rehearsal." This is not a dress rehearsal. We're not going to get to do this again and get it right. If we waste our lives in bitterness or dishonesty or anger or prejudice or self-hatred or envy or selfishness or boredom, it isn't like we're going to get to try again. This is it. And it will end. Someday will be the last day.

To get that truth way down in our bones, and to live as though we believe it, is to become wise the way the psalmist was wise: "Teach us to count our days, so that we may gain a wise heart." Why is it that we almost never become wise the easy way?[4] Almost everyone who becomes wise about the limits of life and awake to the brevity of life only gets wise by way of a tragedy. Why do we have to endure a tragic loss or receive an ominous prognosis or bury a dear friend to wake up, become wise, and live as though someday will be the last day? Why can't something short of a tragedy get our attention, like a sermon, a psalm, a prayer, or a chapter in a book? Why can't we just hear the truth that life is fragile and fleeting and be changed by the truth we hear? Wouldn't it be good if something short of a tragedy could make us wise and wake us up to the fact that every day is sacred because someday is going to be the last day?

Amen.

* * * * *

And so it is with every sweet occurrence
That lends any sense or comfort to our lives.
The ultimate gaze and the final phase
Are pretty hard to recognize.
It will happen for the last time,
And very likely no one will know
when it happened that it stopped happening.
So kiss me every time you go
Against returning so obscure
For even though I think I know a certain thing
I can't be sure.

—*Mary Connell*
Final Sightings

Let us love one another as persons who
could soon be snatched away . . . Let us
all love one another as persons who
could soon be separated.

—*Friedrich Schleiermacher,*
Sermon at Nathanael's Grave

NOTES

[1] Anne Lamott, *Traveling Mercies* (New York: Pantheon Books, 1999), 235.

[2] Thornton Wilder, *Our Town* (New York: Harper and Row, 1938), 97-100.

[3] Mitch Albom, *Tuesdays with Morrie* (New York: Doubleday, 1997), 82.

[4] "Becoming wise the easy way" is an idea that was spawned for me by William Willmon's sermon, "What Time Is It," in *A Chorus of Witnesses*, eds. Thomas G. Long and Cornelius Platinga, Jr. (Grand Rapids: Wm. B. Eerdmans, 1994), 102.

CHAPTER TEN

On Staying Ready

Finally, be strong in the Lord and in the strength of his power. Put on the whole armor of God, so that you may be able to stand against the wiles of the devil. For our struggle is not against enemies of blood and flesh, but against the rulers, against the authorities, against the spiritual forces of evil in the heavenly places. Therefore take up the whole armor of God, so that you may be able to withstand on that evil day, and having done everything, to stand firm. Stand therefore, and fasten the belt of truth around your waist and put on the breastplate of right-eousness. As shoes for your feet put on whatever will make you ready to proclaim the gospel of peace. With all of these, take the shield of faith, with which you will be able to quench all the flaming arrows of the evil one. Take the helmet of salvation, and the sword of the Spirit, which is the word of God.

Pray in the Spirit at all times in every prayer and supplication. To that end keep alert and always persevere in supplication for all the saints. Pray also for me, so that when I speak, a message may be given to me to make known with boldness the mystery of the gospel, for which

> I am an ambassador in chains. Pray that I may declare it
> boldly, as I must speak.
>
> —*Ephesians 6:10-20*

"It's a battle out there. The pressures are great, the stakes are high, and the only way to be ready is to stay ready." That's the bottom line in Ephesians 6. It's easy to miss that single, central message because there are such intriguing issues at the edges of the passage. Ephesians 6:10-20 bursts at the seams with intriguing alternate routes and bypasses (wiles of the devil, forces of evil), but all those interesting images only serve to underscore one single, central message: To live in this world as innocent, honest, simple, faithful followers of Jesus is a battle for which we have to get ready and stay ready, or else we won't be ready to face the hard pressures when they come, because when they come it is almost always with no warning. That's the passionate, urgent message at the center of Ephesians 6.

The writer of Ephesians uses the image of "putting on the armor of God" as a metaphor for getting ready to face the struggles and temptations that come our way. Then, after invoking the image of the armor, he says a simple, straightforward word about being ready: "Pray in the Spirit at all times...keep alert and always persevere in prayer for all the saints." Having begun by saying, "Be strong in the Lord," the passage ends by telling us how to become strong in the Lord: "Pray at all times...keep alert and always keep praying," an admonition that is reminiscent of our Lord's words to the disciples in the Garden of Gethsemane: "Stay awake and pray, that you may not come into the time of trial, for the spirit is willing but the flesh is weak." Jesus knew that unless his friends prayed, they would not be ready for the trials that the coming night would bring. This Ephesian passage seems to say the same thing.

Even if these words weren't in the Bible, we would know that it was so because of what we have learned in our own lives. We know that when we live a life punctuated by frequent and regular times of prayer and devotion, we are far more ready to face whatever comes next. We learned long ago, in the dust and blood of everyday life, that our daily practice of prayer and devotion makes a real difference in how we respond to the routine irritations, trivial frustrations, and dangerous temptations that come to us with no warning. There will always be great mysteries about how God uses prayer to alter the course of events around us, but there is no question that God uses our praying to change us. When we live prayerful lives, we speak differently, spend differently, act differently, decide differently, react and respond and even see differently than when we just rush unprepared through each new day. I don't mean to suggest that a little prayer every morning puts us on an auto-pilot flight of sweetness and light for the rest of the day. That is certainly not so. There are no such simple guarantees. But I do mean to say that the best way for us to stay ready for whatever comes next is to do exactly what this epistle passage says: "Pray in the Spirit at all times . . . keep alert and always persevere in prayer." *Listen for God. Talk with God.* It takes time, energy, and discipline, but that's how we get ready and stay ready for the future.

There are people who actually live that way, people who live what our Quaker friends call "a centered life." They aren't plastic, perfect people. They're ordinary, flesh and blood humans who fall down and get up and struggle and wonder like the rest of us. Except they almost always respond to life's temptations and react to life's frustrations with the kind of strength and patience that makes the rest of us want to be better than we are. Almost all of them got that way because they chose to punctuate their lives with stillness and silence and prayer. They got that way because they chose to saturate their lives with words and images that are pure and good. Somewhere along the way, they decided that the stakes were high enough and life was

49

unpredictable enough that they should "put on the armor of God," which is just another way of saying that they decided they should get ready and stay ready for whatever came next. In the process of staying ready, without them even being aware of it, their lives have become beautiful, so beautiful that "we have to have God to explain them."[1]

It is not too late for the rest of us to choose to live that way. Nor is it too soon. Perhaps we could begin with so simple an act as assuming that our baptism actually means something. Perhaps we could begin by saying, each day, throughout the day, something like this: "Lord, I want to live today as a baptized person, as a person who actually belongs to you, God. I have no idea what struggle or decision or temptation I will face today. But in every case, I want to react and respond as a baptized person should. I want to react and respond and choose and decide in ways that are true and pure and innocent and kind and good. But I am not up to that, O God. So help me. Help me to be ready for whatever is coming next."

That doesn't seem like much, but it is at least a place to start. We have to start somewhere. And we have to start sometime. Now is not too late. But neither is it too soon.

Amen.

* * * * *

It is never too late to become the person you might have been.

—*George Eliot*

NOTE

[1] Slight paraphrase of E. Glenn Hinson, *Love at the Heart of Things* (Wallingford: Pendle Hill Publications, 1998), 91.

CHAPTER ELEVEN

W. W. J. D.

Then he began to teach them that the Son of Man must undergo great suffering, and be rejected by the elders, the chief priests, and the scribes, and be killed, and after three days rise again. He said all this quite openly.
And Peter took him aside and began to rebuke him. But turning and looking at his disciples, he rebuked Peter and said, "Get behind me, Satan! For you are setting your mind not on divine things but on human things."

He called the crowd with his disciples, and said to them, "If any want to become my followers, let them deny themselves and take up their cross and follow me. For those who want to save their life will lose it, and those who lose their life for my sake, and for the sake of the gospel, will save it."

—Mark 8:31-35

Midway through her novel *Wise Blood*, Flannery O'Connor introduces us to Onnie Jay Holy, a street preacher and radio evangelist who tries to draw a crowd by preaching to them about "a new church with a new jesus." Whenever Onnie Jay Holy talks about this "new jesus" in the novel, the word "jesus" begins with a lower case "j." He believes that this new "small-j jesus" has tremendous potential to draw a crowd. "I seen how a new jesus would be more up to date," he says. "I never heard a idear before that had more in it than that one. All it would need is a little promotion."[1] Onnie Jay Holy's assessment of things was probably pretty accurate. A new small-j jesus might be a great deal more attractive than the other Jesus, the old capital-J Jesus who says such hard things as "deny yourself" and "take up your cross."

No matter how you turn them, those words do not have a soft side. There are only hard, heavy edges to those words. If we are looking for a new jesus, a sweet jesus who will not disturb and disrupt our lives, then we'll have to look somewhere outside the Bible. The Jesus of the Bible is the capital-J Jesus who says that the conditions for following him are for us to deny ourselves and take up the cross. Those are the conditions, plain and simple.

But, of course, they aren't plain and simple, because who knows exactly what Jesus meant when he said those hard words? I keep struggling to make those words make sense in some practical way. Here are some possibilities: To "deny yourself" does not mean to despise yourself, to hate yourself, to demean yourself. It can't mean that and be true to the One who said it. But, at the very least, it does mean, "Trust yourself to God and then get on with living a life that is turned outward. Move beyond the conventional wisdom of looking out for yourself and taking care of your own and see the world around you with the compassionate, concerned, caring eyes of Jesus. Get yourself off your hands and put your life, your future, your reputation, your possessions, your comfort, and your security in God's hands. Let go of yourself so that you can take hold of the world that surrounds you." That is where my struggle with those words has taken me.

The one thing we must never do is trim the old capital-J Jesus down to some new small-j jesus to accommodate the limits of our comfort. Far better it would be just to go ahead and say that we aren't ready to take up the cross and deny ourselves. It would be better to say that we know what the gospel demands and we know what following Jesus requires, but we aren't ready for it. That way we will be speaking the truth about ourselves and Jesus. And if we speak the truth about ourselves and Jesus, there is still hope, hope that we might someday actually say "No" to our trimmed-down, Americanized, comfortable small-j jesus so that we can say a real "Yes" to the big-J Jesus who calls us to get ourselves off our hands and give ourselves away for the glory of God and the good of others.

Amen.

* * * * *

Several years ago now I attended a weekend retreat with about seventy other people, where the opening exercise was to tell a story about someone who had been Christ for us in our lives. One after the other, they were stories of comfort, compassion, and rescue. The conference room turned into a church, where we settled into the warmth of each other's company. Jesus our friend was there with us and all was right with the world, until this one woman stood up and said, "Well, the first thing I thought about when I tried to think who had been Christ to me was, 'Who in my life has told me the truth so clearly that I wanted to kill him for it?'" She burst our bubble, but she was onto something vitally important that most of us would be glad to forget: namely, that the Christ is not only the one who comforts and rescues us. The Christ is also the one who challenges and upsets us.

—*Barbara Brown Taylor,* Home By Another Way

NOTE

[1] *Flannery O'Connor: Collected Works* (New York: The Library of America, 1988), 90.

CHAPTER TWELVE

Why the King Came

Then Pilate entered the headquarters again, summoned Jesus, and asked him, "Are you the King of the Jews?" Jesus answered, "Do you ask this on your own, or did others tell you about me?" Pilate replied, "I am not a Jew, am I? Your own nation and the chief priests have handed you over to me. What have you done?" Jesus answered, "My kingdom is not from this world. If my kingdom were from this world, my followers would be fighting to keep me from being handed over to the Jews. But as it is, my kingdom is not from here." Pilate asked him, "So you are a king?" Jesus answered, "You say that I am a king. For this I was born, and for this I came into the world, to testify to the truth. Everyone who belongs to the truth listens to my voice." Pilate asked him, "What is truth?"

—John 18:33-38

Things don't seem to be going all that royally for Christ the King in John 18. By this point in the gospel of John, Jesus had already been arrested and roughly handled. There was a crowd outside clamoring for his execution, and the only thing remaining between Jesus and the cross was his conversation with the Roman governor Pilate. Tucked away in that closing conversation of Jesus' life is one of the clearest statements Jesus ever offered concerning his reason for being in the world. Pilate pressed Jesus on the question of whether or not he was really the King of the Jews, finally asking, "So, are you a king?" Jesus answered, "You say that I am a king. For this I was born, and for this I came into the world, to testify to the truth." That's why Jesus was born, according to Jesus. "For this I was born, and for this I came into the world, to show the world the truth." That is what Christ the King said about why Christ the King came.

Of course, it got him killed . . . telling the truth, I mean. The truth Jesus revealed about who God is, what God wants for us to do, and how God means for us to live was so threatening to the world into which Jesus was born that eventually people had to hush him up, silence him, and do away with him before he turned everything upside down.

Usually, it is right about here that we say something about the Jews rejecting Jesus and first-century Judaism refusing to claim him as Lord. But if we say such words, we should only say them with a soft voice and a repentant heart, partly because of the dreadful way in which such pronouncements have fueled the awful contradiction of Christian anti-Semitism. Christianity has a wonderful history, but that history also holds shameful seasons during which some Christians treated Jews in ways that utterly defy and deny the spirit of Christ, himself a Jew. For that reason alone, if we speak of first-century Judaism rejecting Jesus, it must be "on our knees," in our softest voices with our most repentant hearts.

Another reason why we must only speak of such things in hushed humility is that when it comes to rejecting the truth that Jesus came to tell, first-century Judaism doesn't have a whole lot on twenty-first century Christianity. We Christians don't do much better than they did when it comes to embracing the truth that Jesus came to tell. For example:

Do not resist an evildoer.
If anyone strikes you on the right cheek,
 turn the other also.
If anyone wants to sue you for your coat, give them
 your sweater too.
Give to everyone who begs from you.

That's the kind of truth the king came to tell.

Do not store up for yourselves treasures on earth.
You cannot serve God and serve wealth.
Go, sell your possessions, give the money to the poor
 and then come follow me.
A person's life does not consist in the abundance
 of their possessions.
None of you can become my disciples if you do not
 give up all your possessions.
When you give a luncheon or a dinner, do not invite
 your friends or rich neighbors who can repay you, but
 instead, invite the poor, the crippled, the lame and
 the blind who cannot reciprocate.

That's the kind of truth the king came to tell.

Love your enemies and pray for those who hurt you.

That's the kind of truth the king came to tell.

Recently, I plowed back through all four gospels, looking for the truth that the king came to tell. As I pondered the truth that the king came to tell, it occurred to me that, whenever we hear various Christian denominations describing how many millions of members they have, such vast success may be a sign that we might not have been telling people the exact same truth that Christ the King came to tell. I mean, really now, do you think there are millions of people who are ready to embrace the truth that Christ the King came to tell? *Do not resist evildoers? Sell your possessions and give the proceeds to the poor? If someone sues for a thousand offer them two-thousand? Deny yourself? Give to everyone who begs from you? Love your enemies?* If we had been telling people the truth that Christ the King came to tell, would we really need as many big church buildings as we have in the world? Would we still need crossing-guards to direct the Sunday morning traffic if Christianity actually meant embracing fully the truth that Christ the King came to tell?

It almost seems that there are two versions of Christianity at work in the world. One is the attractive, comfortable, sweet-Jesus version that churches use to get people in, a version of the gospel that doesn't challenge our consumerism or question our materialism, a version of the gospel that allows churches to spend lavishly on their institutional advancement so they can attract bigger crowds and succeed on the terms that North America applauds. Then, there is the steep-Jesus version of the gospel, the gospel of the New Testament, the gospel that reflects the truth that the king came to tell: "Go, sell your possessions, give the money to the poor. Then come follow me. . . . None of you can be my disciples if you do not give up all your possessions. . . . Do not store up for yourselves treasures on earth." If we read the Bible and speak the truth about what we find there, we know that this is the real gospel. The truth the king came to tell is not a sweet-Jesus message of success and comfort that draws a crowd; it is a steep-Jesus message of cross-bearing that calls us to find our joy not in acquisition and clutter, but in spending ourselves for others and in giving ourselves away for those who struggle and hurt. If we "get people saved" with the sweet-Jesus gospel that dangles before them the carrot of comfort and success, when do we pull back the carrot to reveal the cross? At what point do we say, "Oh, by the way, the comfortable buildings and entertaining events and popular activities that we offered to attract you to our church have nothing to do with the real message of the gospel."

The real message is the truth the king came to tell. It goes like this: "Take up your cross. Deny yourself. Love your enemies. Give to everyone who begs from you. None of you can be my disciples if you do not give up all your possessions." When do we break the bad news to the converts who came streaming in under the impression that the gospel would fit in just fine with their North American view of success and comfort? Does it not tell us something that when Jesus himself was telling the truth he was born to tell, he never could keep a crowd? He sometimes had a crowd, but he told such a severe truth that he always lost them. So he lived and died as a largely unclaimed king among his own people, the Jews, and a largely unclaimed king he yet remains among his own people, the Christians.

The weight of all this is enough to take the life out of you. According to Jesus himself, Jesus came to tell the truth, and some of the truth he told so radically shatters our self-centered, protectionist, comfort-obsessed, consumer-driven way of looking at life that we are as threatened by him as the crowd that clamored for his crucifixion. It's enough to make you want to give up, except for the fact that there is also all that other truth that the king came to tell. You know, the part of the truth that actually gives us a reason to believe that we might yet crown Christ King: *Come unto me all you who labor and are heavy laden and I will give you rest . . . Neither do I condemn you, go and sin no more . . . Father forgive them, for*

*they don't know what they are doing . . . Go in peace, your sins
are forgiven.* That too, is the truth the king came to tell. This
truth gives us cause to believe that we might yet crown Christ
King, despite our long history of flinching in the face of the
truth the king came to tell.

Amen.

* * * *

Are you familiar with a little book that Edith Hamilton
wrote toward the end of her life called *Witness to the
Truth*? . . . She said the great church of Christ was
founded by good [people] . . . who loved Christ enough
to die for Him, but they did not trust Christ . . . enough to
build the church by His way of doing things. So they set
about to make it safe in their own way . . . She argued that
the church became strong, it became powerful, and it
became rich, but weaker and weaker until today, it's
hardly distinguishable from any other social organization.

—*Will Campbell, in Susan Ketchin's*
The Christ-Haunted Landscape

CHAPTER THIRTEEN

The Truth at the Bottom of Easter

Now I would remind you, brothers and sisters, of the truth that I proclaimed to you . . .

For I handed on to you as of first importance what I in turn had received; that Christ died for our sins in accordance with the Scriptures and that he was buried, and that he was raised on the third day in accordance with the Scriptures . . .

Therefore, my beloved, be steadfast, immovable, always excelling in the work of the Lord, because you know that in the Lord your labor is not in vain.

—1 Corinthians 15:1-4, 58

I'm a little hesitant to bring this up, but we may as well say it out loud, because if you've been reading your Bible much, you already know it anyway. The fact is, some of Easter's facts don't quite match. If it's a neat, nice, tidy set of matching Easter facts you're after, then take it from me—don't go flipping around from gospel to gospel. Matthew says that two women went to the tomb, John says there was only one, and Mark says that there were three. In Matthew, it appears that the stone is rolled away after the women arrive, but in Mark it is gone before they get there. And, while the other gospels say that the women ran to tell the news of the empty tomb, Mark says they were so afraid that they said nothing to anyone. The fact is, there isn't one carefully harmonized set of matching Easter facts. But beneath the multiple layers of facts and the several voices that report them, there is the truth that waits at the bottom of Easter. Once you peel away the facts at the edges of Easter, what remains is the truth at the bottom of Easter.

In 1 Corinthians 15, Paul assigns the truth at the bottom of Easter to a place at the top of the list: "I would remind you, brothers and sisters, of the good news that I proclaimed to you . . . For I handed on to you as of first importance the truth that I had received: That Christ died for our sins, that he was buried, and that he was raised on the third day." With that introduction, Paul launches into his longest and deepest reflection on the resurrection, which he concludes with the last verse of 1 Corinthians 15, where he says, "Therefore, my beloved, be steadfast, immovable, always excelling in the work of the Lord, because you know that your labor is not in vain." With those words, Paul brings us to the practical side of Easter. With those words, Paul does not tell us something that proves the resurrection as much as he tells us something that the resurrection proves. The resurrection proves that, ultimately, nothing done in the name of our Lord will be wasted, lost, or pointless, because God's goodness and power will ultimately triumph over all that is evil and hurtful and wrong. That is the truth at the bottom of Easter, and it becomes the truth at the center of life when we believe it, embrace it, and draw from it the ethical energy to go about doing the right thing and living for the gospel with the courage that comes from knowing that nothing will be lost or wasted or pointless. "Your labor is not in vain."

Not long ago I stumbled across the story of a man named Jonathan Myrick Daniels. In the spring of 1965, Jonathan Myrick Daniels, a seminary student in Cambridge, Massachusetts, felt that God was calling him to go to Alabama and serve as a volunteer in the struggle for equal rights for all citizens. Once there, he participated in a nonviolent demonstration, which landed him in jail. The day he was released, he was shot to death.[1] Someone who knew Jonathan Myrick Daniels might have thought, "What a waste. He was twenty-six, bright and gifted with a wonderful future in the ministry. And now he's gone; dead for a lost cause." But here we are, nearly forty years later, living in a different world, a world he helped change, and we're still calling his name. "*Your labor is not in vain.*" Nothing is lost, nothing is lost, nothing is lost, because the goodness and truth of God will triumph and prevail. The resurrection proved it first, and the evidence has been mounting ever since.

This is the practical side of Easter. The practical side of Easter is not about the resurrection as a collection of neatly collated facts. The practical side of Easter isn't about the resurrection as a doctrinal plank in orthodoxy's platform. The practical side of Easter is about the resurrection as our source of ethical energy and courage, because we know that if God raised Christ from the grave, then nothing done for God will be lost, wasted, or in vain. The resurrection proves that ultimately, God's goodness and truth will prevail. So we think of God's wonderful children and young people and college students, and we wonder if some of them may grow up and choose to go into politics, where they might courageously lose an election someday because they will choose to speak too clearly on great but unpopular causes, having found the courage to lose for what is right because they learned on Easter Sundays the truth that nothing done for God is done in vain. And others, with all their education and advantages, might choose, from all the professions they could have chosen, to be a nursing home orderly, because they know that the simplest kindness or comfort offered to the weakest of God's children is not in vain in the light of Easter's truth. And some who have resources will give with joy to lift the poor, while others will take up the cause of minorities who could use a majority voice, and still others will catch the eye of every child in the hallway at school and say to them a kind and encouraging word. Some will pray by name for people who will never know it but will someday feel it, and others will make it their life's passion to reach out to the outcast and the embarrassed and the stranger. And they all will know that, in the light of Easter's truth, it all matters and none of it is in vain because of what the resurrection proves. The resurrection proves that a life lived for God, though it may appear to be hidden in obscurity or lost in failure, defeat, and death, is a life not lived in vain because God will make of that life something more than anyone ever dreamed, imagined, or dared to hope.

The truth at the bottom of Easter has a practical side that tells us our labor is not in vain. Nothing is lost, nothing is lost, nothing is lost. That is the truth of which the resurrection is the ultimate demonstration. That is the truth at the bottom of Easter, which makes it the truth at the top of the list. And once you believe it, embrace it, and cast yourself upon it, it really does become the truth at the center of life.

Amen.

*****

Anxiety and fear are what we know best . . . We have heard so much tragic news that when the news is good we cannot hear it. But the proclamation of Easter Day is that all is well . . . In the end, God's will, not ours, is done. Love is the victor. Death is not the end. The end is life . . . Existence has greater depths of beauty, mystery and benediction than the wildest visionary has ever dared to dream. Christ our Lord has risen.

—*Frederick Buechner*
The End Is Life

NOTE

[1] Barbara Brown Taylor, *Home By Another Way* (Boston: Cowley Publications, 1999), 126-127.

CHAPTER FOURTEEN

When Grace Gets Out of Line

When God saw what they did, how they turned from their evil ways, God changed his mind about the calamity that God had said he would bring upon them . . .

But this was very displeasing to Jonah and he became angry. He prayed to the Lord and said, "That is why I fled to Tarshish in the beginning, for I knew that you are a gracious God and merciful, slow to anger and abounding in steadfast love, ready to relent from punishing."

—*Jonah 3:10–4:2*

For the kingdom of heaven is like a landowner who went out early in the morning to hire laborers for his vineyard. After agreeing with the laborers for the usual daily wage, he sent them into his vineyard. When he went out about nine o'clock, he saw others standing idle in the marketplace; and he said to them, "You also go into the vineyard, and I will pay you whatever is right." So they went. When he went out again about noon and about three o'clock, he did the same. And about five o'clock he went out and found others standing around; and he said to them, "Why are you standing here idle all day?" They said to him, "Because no one has hired us." He said to them, "You also go into the vineyard." When evening came, the owner of the vineyard said to his manager, "Call the laborers and give them their pay, beginning with the last and then going to the first." When those hired about five o'clock came, each of them received the usual daily wage. Now when the first came, they thought they would receive more; but each of them also received the usual daily wage. And when they received it, they grumbled against the landowner, saying, "These last worked only one hour, and you have made them equal to us who have borne the burden of the day and the scorching heat." But he replied to one of them, "Friend, I am doing you no wrong; did you not agree with me for the usual daily wage? Take what belongs to you and go; I choose to give to this last the same as I give to you. Am I not allowed to do what I choose with what belongs to me? Or are you envious because I am generous?" So the last will be first, and the first will be last."

—*Matthew 20:1-16*

Sometimes grace gets a little too amazing. Sometimes God is a little too good. If you don't believe it, just ask Jonah. Jonah was angry at God for being too good. God had been better to the Ninevites than Jonah wanted God to be. Jonah despised the people of Nineveh. What he really wanted was for God to zap them. But God showed mercy to the people of Nineve\h, so Jonah was angry. The amazing grace of God was a little too amazing to suit Jonah. As far as Jonah was concerned, when God was merciful to the Ninevites, grace went a little too far. Grace got out of line.

Which is exactly what grace did in Matthew 20. Matthew 20:1-16 is a parable about a payday when grace got out of line, did too much, and went too far. It's a troubling parable, isn't it? As one wise observer has said , "It takes two to parable, one to tell it and one to be upset by it." That is especially true of this parable. Few parables have a capacity to upset us like this one. This story offends our sense of fairness and justice. Those who work twelve hours and those who work one hour all get paid the same amount at the end of the day? How absurd! What sort of labor law is that? This is no way to run a business. Whoever heard of such a thing—paying everybody an all-day wage when some have put in twelve hours and others have worked only one? But, of course, labor-relations and pay-scales are not what the story is about. This parable, as is true of almost all of Jesus' parables, has only one point to make. The details of the story exist only to serve the purpose of setting the stage for that one point to be driven home. To see the single point of this parable, we have to find our way to the final paragraph, where the parable reaches its pinnacle. The all-day workers receive exactly what they contracted for, but they are angry, because even though they got exactly the wage they had agreed upon, those last-minute stragglers received just as much as they, who earned what they got. So here is how it all ends:

> They grumbled against the landowner, saying, "These last worked only one hour, and you have made them equal to us who have borne the burden of the day and the scorching heat." But the landowner replied, "Friend, I am doing you no wrong; did you not agree with me for the usual daily wage? Take what belongs to you and go; I choose to give to this last crowd the same as I give to you. Am I not allowed to do what I choose with what belongs to me? Or are you envious because I am generous?" So the last will be first and the first will be last.

The all day workers were not short-changed. They got everything they were promised. They were properly compensated for their labor—a day's wage for a day's work, which is exactly what they had agreed upon when they climbed in the pick-up that morning. But, nonetheless, they bristled at the landowner because they resented the fact that the undeserving late-comers were the recipients of sheer grace and generosity that equaled what they had earned. When the landowner said, "Are you envious because I am generous?" their answer would have to be, "Yes. Absolutely. We are envious because you are generous. We find your generosity unfair." And, personally, I sort of sympathize with them. I can identify with their dismay. I mean, think about it. You show up at daylight and work all-day and you get twenty dollars. Somebody else shows up at four in the afternoon, works until five, and they also get twenty. It goes against the grain a little bit. Which is no doubt what Jesus intended. He gets our attention and then he tells us what the story means to say about God: "I choose to give to the last the same as I give to you. Am I not allowed to do what I choose with what belongs to me? Are you envious because I am generous?"

There it is. That's what the offensive little story is all about. Grace is God's gift to give, and God can give that grace to anyone or to everyone. Those of us who think we've done enough to earn God's embrace don't have one bit of business determining whom God can embrace. If God wants to embrace people we despise, that's God's business. If God chooses to receive people we reject, that's God's business. If God welcomes into heaven those we don't think should go, that's God's business. We don't have to worry. God's isn't going to keep us out in order to let them in. We'll get everything we were promised. But this parable suggests that those whom we thought shouldn't be as welcome as we are might even get to go in ahead of us. We might be going in behind them. No telling who might be there, because God can give grace to whomever God chooses. In the words of the parable, "Is God not allowed to do what God chooses with what belongs to

God?" Are we envious because God is good? Jonah had to say "Yes. Matter of fact, I am. I didn't want the Ninevites to be saved. Yes, I'd rather they be left out." And the all-day workers in the parable would have to say, "Yes. I'm angry at your generosity. I don't want the late-comers to be made equal to me."

This can be hard for some of us. We see ourselves as the all-day workers who show up and do right and work hard. We actually feel entitled to be loved, blessed, and received by God. But what if the truth is we're all in the late crowd, just the children of grace, saved by grace and nothing else? If we could ever recover our sense of God's grace, we would see ourselves as the late-comers who got more than they deserved, and we would never begrudge any sinner their undeserved welcome into God's home, because we would know that our own welcome was as undeserved as theirs—all of grace, only of grace, entirely of grace. Then we wouldn't have such a need to make sure that, in the end, some are going to be left out. We'd be happy for grace to go too far and to get out of line. But we're not quite there. It's not easy to let go of our sense of entitlement and abandon ourselves to grace. It's hard to bring our own lives in line with the grace that is always getting out of line.

It's sort of like if you received a beautiful engraved card inviting you to a very fancy party. You had been hoping you would be on the invitation list, because you knew that this was going to be quite a lavish event. Then, with great excitement, you arrive at the party and it turns out to be just as wonderful as you imagined. There are bands, flowers, linen, silver, mountains of boiled shrimp, and oceans of red punch, and it is truly the nicest party you've ever been to. But you are not as happy about the party as you thought you would be. You can't really enjoy it because you had been thinking that you were among a privileged group of special people who had been invited, but now that you're there, you discover that your host invited everybody in town. There's plenty of room for everyone, and more than enough food to go around. But somehow, it doesn't feel quite the same, now that you know that anybody can come in and be welcome at the party. You know you should be able to enjoy the party, but you can't.

That's sort of the way it is when our lives aren't in line with the radical grace of God that is always going too far and getting out of line to include people that we never dreamed would be part of the party! We'll have to get over that, or we might not enjoy heaven. (You know, too many people there; people we didn't think would be invited.)

Amen.

*****

There was only a purple streak in the sky, cutting through a field of crimson and leading, like an extension of the highway, into the descending dusk. Mrs. Turpin saw the streak as a vast swinging bridge extending upward from the earth through a field of living fire. Upon it a vast horde of souls were rumbling toward heaven. There were whole companies of white-trash, clean for the first time in their lives . . . and battalions of freaks and lunatics shouting and clapping and leaping like frogs. And bringing up the end of the procession was a tribe of people whom she recognized at once as those who, like herself and Claud, had always had a little of everything and the God-given wit to use it right. She leaned forward to observe them closer. They were marching behind the others with great dignity, accountable as they had always been for good order and common sense and respectable behavior. They alone were on key. Yet she could see by their shocked and altered faces that even their virtues were being burned away.

—*Mrs. Turpin's vision of glory, in*
Flannery O'Connor's short story "Revelation"

CHAPTER FIFTEEN

Where God Draws the Line 16-13

Now all the tax collectors and sinners were coming near to listen to him. And the Pharisees and the scribes were grumbling and saying, "This fellow welcomes sinners and eats with them."

So he told them this parable: . . . "There was a man who had two sons. The younger of them said to his father, 'Father, give me the share of the property that will belong to me.' So he divided his property between them. A few days later the younger son gathered all he had and traveled to a distant country, and there he squandered his property in dissolute living. When he had spent everything, a severe famine took place throughout that country, and he began to be in need. So he went and hired himself out to one of the citizens of that country, who sent him to his fields to feed the pigs. He would gladly have filled himself with the pods that the pigs were eating; and no one gave him anything. But when he came to himself he said, 'How many of my father's hired hands have bread enough and to spare, but here I am dying of hunger! I will get up and go to my father, and I will say to him, "Father, I have sinned against heaven and before you; I am no longer worthy to be called your son; treat me like one of your hired hands.'" So he set off and went to his father. But while he was still far off, his father saw him and was filled with compassion; he ran and kissed him. Then the son said to him, 'Father, I have sinned against heaven and before you; I am no longer worthy to be called your son.' But the father said to his slaves, 'Quickly, bring out a robe—the best one—and put it on him; put a ring on his finger and sandals on his feet. And get the fatted calf and kill it, and let us celebrate; for this son of mine was dead and is alive again; he was lost and is found!' And they began to celebrate.

"Now his elder son was in the field; and when he came and approached the house, he heard music and dancing. He called one of the slaves and asked what was going on. He replied, 'Your brother has come, and your father has killed the fatted calf, because he has got him back safe and sound.' Then he became angry and refused to go in. His father came out and began to plead with him. But he answered his father, 'Listen! For all these years I have been working like a slave for you, and I have never disobeyed your command; yet you have never given me even a young goat so that I might celebrate with my friends. But when this son of yours came back, who has devoured your property with prostitutes, you killed the fatted calf for him!' Then the father said to him, 'Son, you are always with me, and all that is mine is yours. But we had to celebrate and rejoice, because this brother of yours was dead and has come to life; he was lost and has been found'."

—*Luke 15:1-3, 11-32*

What do you suppose this story meant the first time it was told? On that long-ago day when Jesus actually told the story we call "the parable of the prodigal son," what point do you think Jesus meant to make? Since the time the story was first told, we have called upon it to mean many things. Indeed, rarely has any one story been turned to to fill so many roles. Of course, the reason we press this story into so many duties is because it raises so many issues. It has one adult child paying a price for another adult child's immaturity. It has parents loving their children equally, but not treating them identically, because their needs are not identical. It raises the issue of how and when and if parents should step in to rescue their children from the tough consequences of poor choices. All of that, and more, is tucked away in the parable of the prodigal son, so it is no surprise that we press the parable into the service of so many different dilemmas.

But, while all of that is extremely important, none of that is exactly what the now-famous story was about the first time it got told. Our best clue to the original point of the parable probably lies a few verses above the place where the story begins, back at the beginning of Luke 15 where the Bible says, "Now all the tax collectors and sinners were coming near to listen to Jesus. And the Pharisees and scribes were grumbling and saying, 'This fellow welcomes sinners and eats with them.' So Jesus told them this parable . . . ." Those opening verses of Luke 15 give us our best clue to the point Jesus was trying to make when he told the story we call "the parable of the prodigal son." The scribes and Pharisees grumbled because Jesus welcomed real sinners. Instead of rejoicing to see sinners at Jesus' table, they were offended, angered, and unhappy. And it was at that moment, when they were complaining about Jesus' wide welcome, that Jesus said, "Let me tell you a story." In response to the Pharisees and scribes who grumbled over Jesus' indiscriminate welcome of known sinners, Jesus told the now-famous story about how God's circle of welcome embraces those who are most broken, most hopeless, and most helpless.

The scribes and Pharisees were not bad people. They were, in fact, good people—good people who sincerely believed that they knew where the line should be drawn, where the circle of God's welcome should stop. That's why they grumbled when Jesus welcomed sinners. They honestly believed that Jesus had crossed the line. So Jesus told them the story to show them that their circle was too small. Jesus told them the story to show them that where they drew the line was not as far out as where God draws the line. They are the elder brother in the story, the person who cannot rejoice over the wide open welcome of a real, sure-enough sinner. They draw their line too soon. God draws the line somewhere further out than they have ever even imagined. That was the point of the story. That's what the story was about the first time it got told: God's big circle, God's wide embrace, God's astounding welcome of broken, flawed, sinful people.

What the story said to them, it says to us. When it comes to "who's in" and "who's out," we draw the line one place, and God draws the line somewhere else. When it comes to who gets welcomed into God's family, our line most always lands somewhere inside God's line. The arc of our circle is rarely as wide as God's. God's got a mighty big circle. That's the point of the story. There was a certain man who had *two* sons—and loving one didn't mean leaving the other.

God's circle of welcome is almost always bigger than ours. Exactly how much bigger is something we will probably never fully realize until we get to heaven and see who all else has been welcomed home. So we should probably go ahead now and get used to the fact that where God draws the line is somewhere outside where we draw the line. We may as well go ahead and get used to it, and get happy about it. Otherwise, we may be unhappy in, of all places, heaven. (And that would be a very long time to be unhappy!)

Amen.

* * * * *

The common thought is that there must be losers if there are winners. Hence, even in religion, it is very difficult not to think Jews or Gentiles, poor or rich, saint or sinner, older son or younger son. But God's love is both/and, not either/or.

—Fred Craddock, concerning the parable
of the prodigal son in his commentary on Luke

CHAPTER SIXTEEN

What Should We Make of the Open Gate?

Do not remember the former things,
   or consider the things of old.
I am about to do a new thing;
      now it springs forth, do you not perceive it?
I will make a way in the wilderness
      and rivers in the desert.
The wild animals will honor me,
      the jackals and the ostriches;
for I give water in the wilderness,
      rivers in the desert,
to give drink to my chosen people,
      the people whom I formed for myself
      so that they might declare my praise.

Yet you did not call upon me, O Jacob;
      but you have been weary of me, O Israel!
You have not brought me your sheep for burnt offerings,
      or honored me with your sacrifices.
I have not burdened you with offerings,
      or wearied you with frankincense.
You have not bought me sweet cane with money,

or satisfied me with the fat of your sacrifices.
But you have burdened me with your sins;
>you have wearied me with your iniquities.

I, I am He
>who blots out your transgressions for my own sake,
>and I will not remember your sins.

—Isaiah 43:18-25

Then one of the seven angels who had the seven bowls full of the seven last plagues came and said to me, "Come, I will show you the bride, the wife of the Lamb." And in the spirit he carried me away to a great, high mountain and showed me the holy city Jerusalem coming down out of heaven from God. It has the glory of God and a radiance like a very rare jewel, like jasper, clear as crystal. It has a great, high wall with twelve gates, and at the gates twelve angels, and on the gates are inscribed the names of the twelve tribes of the Israelites; on the east three gates, on the north three gates, on the south three gates, and on the west three gates.

I saw no temple in the city, for its temple is the Lord God the Almighty and the Lamb. And the city has no need of sun or moon to shine on it, for the glory of God is its light, and its lamp is the Lamb. The nations will walk by its light, and the kings of the earth will bring their glory into it. Its gates will never be shut by day—and there will be no night there. People will bring into it the glory and the honor of the nations. But nothing unclean will enter it, nor anyone who practices abomination or falsehood, but only those who are written in the Lamb's book of life.

—Revelation 21:9-13, 22-25

Is God ever completely, fully, finally done with anyone? Or does God always have something else, something more, something new yet to do? From the Old Testament Lamentation that says God's mercies are new every morning, to the New Testament Revelation that promises God will make all things new, to this beautiful passage in which Isaiah declares, "Thus says the Lord, 'I am about to do a new thing,'" wherever you look in the Bible, God is up to something new. God always has something new, something else, something more yet to come. Apparently, it is just God's nature never to be finished with anything or through with anybody.

One has to figure that if God was ever going to give up on someone, it might have been the people to whom God spoke through Isaiah. God says to them, "You have burdened me with your sins and you have wearied me with your transgressions." That is a capsule synopsis of such longer litanies as this one from Isaiah: "Listen, O earth, for the Lord has spoken: I reared children and brought them up, but they have rebelled against me. They are laden with iniquity, they do evil, they deal corruptly, they have forsaken the Lord and despised the Holy One of Israel." And this one from Hosea: "When Israel was a child I loved him, and out of Egypt I called my child, but the more I called them, the more they went away from me, sacrificing to false gods and burning incense to idols. They are determined to turn away from me." And this one from Amos: "I know how many are your transgressions and how great are your sins—you trample the poor and you push aside the needy." And yet, God is not finished with God's people. God still has this wonderful future in mind for them: "I am about to do a new thing," God says, "I am the one who blots out your transgressions for my own sake, and I will not remember your sins."

This, apparently, is the way God is. Apparently, it is God's nature to keep doing something new, to keep going forward, opening new chapters, giving new chances, creating new opportunities for people to become what God has created them to become, no matter how miserably or consistently we have failed to live as God's people. If that sounds a little too warm and fuzzy, a little too soft and lenient, then listen to the conclusion of Isaiah's message: "You have burdened me with your sins and you have wearied me with your iniquities, but I am the One who blots out your transgressions for my own sake, and I will not remember your sins." God does not wink at their sins. God takes their sin very seriously. In fact, God says, "You have wearied me with your sins." Nor does God swoop in to spare them from the consequences of their sins. God's people have been defeated in battle and carried away captive, where they remain at the time of Isaiah's writing. God takes their choices seriously, seriously enough to let them endure the consequences of their choices. And yet, God still has more in mind for them. God will yet do a new and wonderful thing for them because that is just the way God is. In fact, God isn't even holding onto them for their sake, but for God's sake. Isaiah 43:25 says, "I am the One who blots out your transgression for my own sake." God will not abandon, reject, or cast away God's children—not only for their sake, but for God's own sake as well. Despite everything, God will yet do a new thing.

It would appear that God is never done with anyone. God keeps making new—making new chances for us and making new people of us until our lives declare praise to God. That is the predominant witness of Scripture. That is the gospel of God, the good story about the way God is. I believe it is true. I believe it is the fundamental truth at the center of the universe, at the top of the heavens, and at the bottom of life. If we ever hit bottom, I believe that what we will find at the bottom will be God, eager to do something new with us and for us, because that just seems to be the way God is.

I wonder if that might be why all those gates were left open. You know, those twelve gates that punctuate the wall surrounding the city of God, the gates of pearl. The last page of the Bible says that those gates never close. God's got gates, a whole dozen of them. But God never closes even one of them. According to Revelation chapter twenty-one, God's gates have been left open . . . forever.

What might that mean? Of course, we mustn't make too much of a dozen gates of pearl, perpetually propped open. After all, the very next verse in Revelation speaks about outer darkness and ultimate separation and severe judgment. We must take those severe words seriously. To ignore those words is to fail to speak the truth about the Bible. On the other hand, we wouldn't want to assign too little meaning to twelve gates left open forever by God. What if they are a sign . . . a dozen signs of something we have yet to learn about the gospel of God?

We must walk softly and speak quietly when we come near those gates left open. To make too little of them or too much of them would leave us in the awkward position of minding God's business, because those gates are God's, not ours.

Amen.

* * * * *

I regret that last term, when that golden opportunity was mine, that I did not give up and become a Christian. It is not now too late . . . but it is hard for me to give up the world.

—*Emily Dickinson in her*
Mount Holyoke journal

CHAPTER SEVENTEEN

On Not Minding God's Business

He put before them another parable: "The kingdom of heaven may be compared to someone who sowed good seed in his field; but while everybody was asleep, an enemy came and sowed weeds among the wheat, and then went away. So when the plants came up and bore grain, then the weeds appeared as well. And the slaves of the householder came and said to him, 'Master, did you not sow good seed in your field? Where, then, did these weeds come from?' He answered, 'An enemy has done this.' The slaves said to him, 'Then do you want us to go and gather them?' But he replied, 'No; for in gathering the weeds you would uproot the wheat along with them. Let both of them grow together until the harvest; and at harvest time I will tell the reapers, Collect the weeds first and bind them in bundles to be burned, but gather the wheat into my barn.'" Then he left the crowds and went into the house. And his disciples approached him, saying, "Explain to us the parable of the weeds of the field." He answered, "The one who sows the good seed is the Son of Man; the field is the world, and the good seed are the children of the kingdom; the weeds are the

> children of the evil one, and the enemy who sowed them
> is the devil; the harvest is the end of the age, and the
> reapers are angels. Just as the weeds are collected and
> burned up with fire, so will it be at the end of the age.
> The Son of Man will send his angels, and they will collect
> out of his kingdom all causes of sin and all evildoers, and
> they will throw them into the furnace of fire, where there
> will be weeping and gnashing of teeth. Then the righteous
> will shine like the sun in the kingdom of their Father. Let
> anyone with ears listen!"
>
> —*Matthew 13:24-30, 36-43*

The parable of the wheat and the weeds is a story that appears, at first glance, to be about an episode of clandestine agricultural sabotage. But, of course, the story is not about farming at all. It is about judging and separating. It is a story about the truth that judgment is ultimately, finally, God's business—not ours. Sort of a companion to Matthew 7:1, "Judge not that you be not judged."

But it's not quite that simple, because Matthew's gospel also says that the church does have a responsibility to make judgments about the lives of its members. In fact, Matthew 18:15-18 provides a formula for confronting wayward church members, a plan of confrontation with a hope for reconciliation but with a provision for separation as a last resort. Such talk as this does not rest easy on our ears. We tend to see sin as a personal matter between an individual and God. Most of us prefer a sort of "live and let live" approach to sin and forgiveness. And anyway, we've heard too many sad tales of legalistic, authoritarian church leaders and graceless excommunication by self-righteous elders. One of my late father's favorite stories was of the long-ago Sunday morning when one of our relatives got reprimanded by his church for, and I quote, "cussing his mule, excessive." (One can only assume that a moderate cussing of the mule would have drawn no sanction. Unless, of course, the accursed mule's name was "Excessive.") One doubts that such sins were on the mind of Matthew when he quoted Jesus' formula for church discipline, but the fact is, the church, in Matthew's gospel, is a community of faith in which the responsibility of making judgments cannot be dodged in the name of "being nice to each other."

But that has to be balanced with the story of the weeds and the wheat, which calls for patient waiting on God to do the judging and separating. The story's point is pretty clear: If we start trying to decide who is in the kingdom and who is not, we will make some wrong judgments. In our zeal to pull up some weeds, we will hurt some wheat. The point the parable makes is that judgment, ultimately, is God's business. When it comes to saying who does or does not belong in the kingdom of heaven, that's God's business, not ours. That is what the parable says in Matthew 13:24-30.

I wish the passage ended there, but it doesn't. The parable is assigned a commentary in Matthew 13:36-43, and the commentary constitutes a fearful paragraph. Without the lectionary to hold our feet to the fire, we might never take it up, because it forces us to struggle with the dark mystery we call "hell" when it says, "The weeds are the children of the evil one, the harvest is the end of the age. At the end of the age, the Son of Man will send his angels, and they will collect all causes of sin and all evildoers, and they will throw them into the furnace of fire, where there will be weeping and gnashing of teeth." We tend to say that this is about hell, and that those who go to hell are those who did not trust in Jesus as their Savior and Lord. It is not so neat though, in Matthew's gospel. Matthew lists other reasons why people go to what we call "hell." In Matthew 8:12, those who are cast into "outer darkness where there will be weeping and gnashing of teeth" are those who arrogantly assumed that they were the rightful heirs of the kingdom of God. In Matthew 24:51, it is the hypocrites who will weep and gnash their teeth. In Matthew 25, it is those who refuse to feed the hungry, clothe the naked, help the sick, welcome the stranger and visit the prison who go away into eternal punishment. In Matthew 13, it is the general category of "evil-doers" who are cast into a furnace of fire to weep and gnash their teeth. It's hard to know what to do with all this, isn't it? What we have traditionally done with it is to say, "Those who don't accept Jesus as their Savior go to hell. Everybody else goes to heaven." That is considered to be standard, orthodox Christianity. But let's be honest. That doesn't fully take into account the complexity of what the gospels say when you run the risk of actually reading them. If we read the Bible and speak the truth, we have to admit that it isn't quite that clear. There is mystery. In the face of that mystery, and in the light of the great, saving grace of God, some say that the notion of hell is just a relic of the three-story worldview of ancient cultures. And yet, the witness of Scripture points, many times, to a real judgment that includes separation between those who have given themselves to God and those who have refused God's grace and God's call.

It's hard to struggle with all this. This is one of those places where it is not easy to read the Bible and speak the truth. If hell is what traditional theology says, an endless fire where people are tormented forever and ever and ever, then that is out of character with everything else we know about God. God's chastisement, punishment, and discipline always have the goal of redeeming, restoring, and reconciling, not inflicting endless pain to settle the score. Endless torment, perpetual punishment with no redemption as its purpose, is out of character with everything else we believe about God. Here, reading the Bible and speaking the truth places us in a tough spot. To say that hell is endless torment will force us to say something that seems unworthy of God. On the other hand, to say, "There is no hell" is to ignore much of what the New

Testament says. To say, "There is a hell, but even there, God's goal is redemption, not torment," is to walk outside the lines of orthodox Christianity. And to make matters worse, it's almost impossible to ponder any of this out loud without being labeled as a fundamentalist on one hand, or a universalist on the other. Nobody ever gets to say an honest "I'm not sure" in the face of all this mystery without being categorized as something by someone who finds mystery an unacceptable confession in the face of the most unknown mystery of all.

Over the long years of my mostly silent struggle to discern the truth about judgment and hell, I have stumbled across some unforgettable insights from others. Among them, this sobering sentence: "The reality of hell is the ultimate testimony to how seriously God takes our freedom."[1] And this daring perspective: "The reality of hell must be acknowledged, as also must the possibility that hell will someday be empty."[2] Third, and finally, the clearest, simplest, best word I have ever encountered about judgment is this from Frederick Buechner: "The One who is going to judge us most finally is the same One who has always loved us most fully."[3] Our sins bring dreadful consequences now, and we await an accounting before God on the Day of Judgment. When that day comes, the One who will judge us most finally is the same One who knows us most intimately, understands us most completely, and loves us most fully. That much, we all know is true. Everything else about Judgment Day is, according to the parable, God's business, not ours.

Amen.

* * * * *

There are important reasons for holding to a doctrine of hell, not least of which is its prominence in the New Testament. . . . On the other hand, there are also passages that would seem to hold out the prospect of ultimate universal redemption.

There is no way to synthesize all these passages. Those that indicate the possibility of being lost for all eternity exist side-by-side with those that indicate God's will, and God's ability, to save all humanity. The reality of hell must be acknowledged, as also must the possibility that ultimately hell will be empty.

—*L. Gregory Jones*
Embodying Forgiveness

NOTES

[1] I saw this sentence in an unpublished sermon by John Claypool.
[2] L. Gregory Jones, *Embodying Forgiveness* (Grand Rapids MI: Wm. B. Eerdmans, 1995), 254.
[3] Frederick Buechner, *Listening to Your Life* (New York: Harper Collins, 1992), 58.

CHAPTER EIGHTEEN

What Grace Is Not

Once more Jesus spoke to them in parables, saying: "The Kingdom of heaven may be compared to a king who gave a wedding banquet for his son.He sent his slaves to call those who had been invited to the wedding banquet,but they would not come. Again he sent other slaves, saying, 'Tell those who have been invited:Look, I have prepared my dinner, my oxen and my fat calves have been slaughtered,and everything is ready; come to the wedding banquet.' But they made light of it and went away, one to his farm, another to his business, while the rest seized his slaves,mistreated them, and killed them. The king was enraged. He sent his troops, destroyed those murderers, and burned their city. Then he said to his slaves, 'The wedding is ready, but those invited were not worthy. Go therefore into the main streets, and invite everyone you find to the wedding banquet.' Those slaves went out into the streets and gathered all whom they found, both good and bad; so the wedding hall was filled with guests.

But when the king came in to see the guests, he noticed a man there who was not wearing a wedding robe, and he said to him, 'Friend, how did you get in

> here without a wedding robe?' And he was speechless.
> Then the king said to the attendants, 'Bind him hand and
> foot, and throw him in the outer darkness, where there
> will be weeping and gnashing of teeth.' For many are
> called, but few are chosen."
>
> —*Matthew 22:1-14*

Talk about snatching defeat from the jaws of victory! That poor soul was seated at the banquet table, napkin in lap, fork in hand, when all of a sudden he got ejected from the dining hall for being improperly attired. (Sort of gives new meaning to that old warning, "no shirt, no shoes, no service.") It's hard to know exactly what to make of this parable. It's a little too heavy, a little too harsh, a little too much to take in.

It's easy to get bogged down in the details of the story. After all, who would kill a servant who just came by to remind them to come to a party? And how could a king wage war on his ungrateful guest list while dinner was on the table? (One imagines that, in the time it would take to mobilize the military, the gravy might thicken.) And what about the poor soul who got tossed before the salad. How was he to know the dress code? He was just pulled in off the street at the last minute, and now he is cast, not just back on the street from whence he came, but into outer darkness to weep and gnash his teeth, all because he wasn't wearing a wedding robe at a wedding feast he hadn't even planned to attend. How unfair is that? Well, you see what I mean. (Smart preachers plan to be vacationing when this parable is on the lectionary itinerary.) There are plenty of places to get bogged down in this story, which is why we have to remember it is a *story*. It is a story about what the grace of God gives and demands. It is a story about what grace is and about what grace is not. We get a glimpse of what grace is in verses nine and ten: *The king said, "Go into the main streets, and invite everyone you find to the wedding banquet." So the slaves went out into the streets and gathered all whom they found, both good and bad, so the wedding hall was filled with guests.* That's a pretty good glimpse of what God's grace is. It is the great embrace, the joyful welcome, the glad reception, the indiscriminate invitation, and the wide acceptance. The wedding hall was filled with guests. (Both good and bad, Matthew is careful to say.) This is a great glimpse of grace. But, if verses nine and ten give us a thrilling look at what grace is, verses eleven through fourteen give us a jarring look at what grace is not:

> When the king came in to see the guests, he noticed a man there who was not wearing a wedding robe, and he said to him, "Friend, how did you get in here without a wedding robe?" And the man was speechless. Then the king said to the attendants, "Bind him hand and foot, and throw him into outer darkness, where there will be weeping and gnashing of teeth." For many are called, but few are chosen.

The message being, apparently, that grace is not just a thrilling gift; it is also a stunning demand. Grace is not a license to act in any way we please; it is instead a call to conform our lives to the values and ideals of the kingdom of God. Grace is not to be presumed upon by those who have received it and been received by it. That appears to be the message of the parable. The parable is not about banquets or dress codes or outer darkness. The parable is ultimately a story about what grace is not. It is a warning to those who might see grace as an easy permissiveness, all gift and no demand.

I recently read a sermon on this parable. It is in a book called *Unleashing the Scripture* by Duke University theologian Stanley Hauerwas. The sermon is called, "You Are **Not** Accepted." It is Dr. Hauerwas' answer to Paul Tillich's famous sermon on grace, "You Are Accepted," generally regarded to be one of the most significant sermons of the twentieth century. In his famous sermon, Paul Tillich called on all people to accept the fact that we are accepted by God. He saw that as the only way for us to overcome our alienation from God. Give up the fight and just accept the fact that God accepts you. That was Paul Tillich's message in his sermon, "You Are Accepted." In his sermon, "You Are **Not** Accepted," Professor Hauerwas praises Tillich's sermon as a needed word and a stirring affirmation of the great truth that God's grace is greater than our sin. But he then goes on to point out that, in Matthew 22, we get the sense that there is "more to this grace thing than simply being accepted." [1] Hauerwas takes us back to the image we encountered in the parable when he says that our wedding garment is the new life we put on at our baptism, "the clothes of righteousness that come from being made citizens of God's kingdom." He concludes his sermon with these memorable words:

> Without the [clothes of righteousness] the news of our acceptance is not good news, but bad news, for who wants to be accepted just as we are? The good news is that by being made part of God's people through immersion in the fire and water of baptism, we are made anew. We can therefore come to God's [banquet] dressed in the wedding garments of our baptism . . . clothed with the ideals of the kingdom of God.

So, which affirmation is most near to the truth—the one that says "You are accepted" or the one that says "You are **not** accepted"? The temptation, of course, is to average them together, making what grace gives a little less thrilling and what grace demands a little less stunning. Why not let them both be what they are? Grace gives everything: acceptance, forgiveness, mercy, salvation. It is God's gift. Believe it. Trust it. Accept it. And grace demands everything: honesty, integrity, generosity, gentleness. Face it, acknowledge it, submit to it, practice it. Grace is not permission to live just any old way we feel. *The grace that gives everything to us demands everything from us.* As it has been put another way, *God loves us so much that God receives us as we are, and God loves us too much to let us remain as we are.*[2]

Grace is a thrilling gift, and it is also a stunning demand. Perish the thought that we would average the two together into something manageable. We must let the gift be as thrilling as it is, and we must let the demand be as stunning as it is. Such is the radical nature of the grace of God, which gives all and demands all.

Amen.

*****

None of us can presume [upon] God's forgiveness regardless of the lives we lead. Rather, each and every one of us must show that we trust in God's forgiveness . . by our pursuit of holiness in an ever-deepening friend-ship with God.

—*L. Gregory Jones,*
Embodying Forgiveness

NOTE

[1] Stanley Hauerwas, *Unleashing the Scripture* (Nashville: Abingdon Press, 1993), 83.

[2] A saying of undetermined origin, but not original with me.

CHAPTER NINETEEN

Late Limbs and Crumb-Catchers

> But now thus says the Lord,
> he who created you, O Jacob,
> he who formed you, O Israel:
> Do not fear, for I have redeemed you;
> I have called you by name, you are
> mine.
> When you pass through the waters, I
> will be with you;
> and through the rivers, they shall
> not overwhelm you;
> when you walk through fire you shall
> not be burned,
> and the flame shall not
> consume you.
> For I am the Lord your God,
> the Holy One of Israel, your Savior.
>
> *—Isaiah 43:1-3*

Jesus left that place and went away to the district of Tyre and Sidon. Just then a Canaanite woman from that region came out and started shouting, "Have mercy on me,

Lord, Son of David; my daughter is tormented by a demon." But he did not answer her at all. And his disciples came and urged him, saying, "Send her away, for she keeps shouting after us." He answered, "I was sent only to the lost sheep of the house of Israel." But she came and knelt before him, saying, "Lord, help me." He answered, "It is not fair to take the children's food and throw it to the dogs." She said, "Yes, Lord, yet even the dogs eat the crumbs that fall from their masters' table." Then Jesus answered her, "Woman, great is your faith! Let it be done for you as you wish." And her daughter was healed instantly.

—*Matthew 15:21-28*

When we Christians read Isaiah 43, we are eavesdropping on what was once said to someone else; something so wonderful that we want to believe it could also be about us; something so hopeful that we need to know it could also be for us:

Do not be afraid, for I have redeemed you. I have called you by name, you are mine. When you pass through the waters I will be with you, and through the rivers they shall not overwhelm you; when you walk through fire you shall not be burned and the flame shall not consume you. For I am the Lord your God, the Holy One of Israel. You are precious in my sight, and I love you. Do not be afraid, for I am with you.

That is the wonderful word we overheard. But it did not first come addressed to us. When Isaiah wrote, "Thus says the Lord, 'Do not fear, for I have redeemed you, I have called you by name, you are mine,'" he was writing to the people of God who had been carried away captive to Babylon. When Isaiah wrote, "Thus says the Lord, 'When you pass through the waters, I will be with you and when you walk through fire you will not be burned,'" he was writing to the people of Israel who had been

LATE LIMBS AND CRUMB-CATCHERS

displaced from their homeland. It is to those people that these wonderful words were spoken. In fact, in the early verses of Isaiah's glorious report of God's word to the captives, Isaiah says, "Thus says the Lord who created you, O Jacob and formed you, O Israel . . . I am the Lord your God, the Holy One of Israel." This beautiful, wonderful, hopeful string of promises was clearly, plainly, particularly given to the people of God who began as the children of Abraham, journeyed to Egypt when Joseph was alive, became Pharaoh's slaves after Joseph's death, and then left Egypt with Moses and wandered in the wilderness.

These people of God finally came into the promised land where they lived until the Babylonians came and carried many of them away by force and kept them as exiles. While they were exiles in Babylon, Isaiah wrote to them those magnificent words, in which God said to them, "Don't be afraid. You are mine. You belong to me. When you pass through the most terrible floods and most awful flames I will be with you. You are precious to me and I love you." And they did come home. They came back home from Babylon and they settled in the part of the promised land called Judah, where they built their faith around the Torah, the laws and words of God. While they were living in exile, their faith came to be called Judaism, and they came to be called the Jews. One day one of their priests named Zechariah and his wife Elizabeth had a baby named John who was a wild, wooly, rough, and rugged Jew who went around saying that the Kingdom of God was coming near and people better get ready. He said one way to show that they were serious about getting ready was to come get wet in the river. Lots of people came to be baptized, and one day a certain Jew came down to the river, and when he came up from the water God said, "This one is my beloved Son, with whom I am well pleased." When he left the river, he began calling people to follow him and that, of course, is where we came in.

So, I guess you could say we came late. Paul's way of putting it in Romans 11 was to say that the Jews are the root and we are the later branches that were grafted in. Jesus' way of putting it was to say that we are the crumb-catchers beneath the table. I know it's not what we want to hear, but in a conversation with a Gentile woman who appealed for his help, Jesus said that he had come for Israel, to the people called the Jews. The woman responded by saying that she realized the Jews had priority, but even the dogs beneath the table got to have the leftovers. And the Bible says that Jesus was so impressed by her analogy that he gave her the help she sought. The crumb-catchers in that story are we non-Jews. In Romans we're the late limbs on God's tree. In Matthew, we're the crumb-catchers beneath God's table.

We came late. It's a miracle that we got in. But, by the grace of God, we did. We are in. We belong to God. We don't have to face the floods and fires alone. God loves us, claims us, calls us by our name, and goes with us through our worst, darkest struggles.

That's what God said to the Jews way back in Isaiah. Some time later, the rest of us were brought in on the same promise. We might have come to the table late, catching fallen crumbs, but now we too belong to God.

Amen.

* * * * *

I didn't know quite what to do with the fact that Jesus had been Jewish. It was a source of pride that someone so esteemed by my Boyd classmates and half the entire world was Jewish. As Jesus' life progressed, however, he somehow ceased to be a practicing Jew and became a Christian. At least that was my understanding.

—*from Edward Cohen's memoir,*
The Peddler's Grandson: Growing Up Jewish in Mississippi

CHAPTER TWENTY

From Luke Two to Two Thousand

After eight days had passed, it was time to circumcise the child; and he was called Jesus . . .

When the time came for their purification according to the law of Moses, they brought him up to Jerusalem . . and they offered a sacrifice according to what is stated in the law of the Lord . . .

Now there was a man in Jerusalem named Simeon; this man was righteous and devout, looking forward to the consolation of Israel, and the Holy Spirit rested on him . . . Guided by the Spirit, Simeon came into the temple; and when the parents brought in the child Jesus, to do for him what was customary under the law, Simeon took him in his arms and praised God, saying,

"Master, now you are dismissing your
            servant in peace,
        according to your word;
    for my eyes have seen your salvation,
        which you have prepared in the
            presence of all peoples,
        a light for revelation to the Gentiles
        and for glory to your people Israel."

—Luke 2:21-40

In his powerful memoir, *The Peddler's Grandson*, Edward Cohen recalls his life as a Jewish child growing up in Jackson, Mississippi. An especially poignant part of the book is Cohen's recollection of his school days, especially the annual fifth-grade Christmas pageant, which created quite a dilemma for a Jewish child who wanted desperately to fit in. In a remarkable paragraph, Edward Cohen writes, "When I was ten, the teacher announced that there would be a Christmas pageant and asked who wanted to participate. . . . That night, when I brought up the Christmas pageant to my parents . . . the ruling of the family Sanhedrin Jewish court was that I could not play Jesus or any of the major figures. I could work backstage, or, if absolutely necessary, I could play a rock or other inanimate object. I didn't know how to explain these fine casting differences to my teacher," Cohen concluded, "so I opted for pulling the curtains. *I stayed hidden, while on stage all the Jewish roles were played by Christians.*"[1]

Edward Cohen was right. All the big roles in the Christmas story (Mary, Joseph, and Jesus) are Jewish roles. In fact, to see just how Jewish are all the main parts in the Christmas story, one need look no further than Luke 2. Luke means to make sure that no one forgets that Jesus was born a very Jewish baby into a very Jewish home. Luke 2:22 says, "When the time came for their purification according to the law of Moses, Mary and Joseph brought Jesus up to Jerusalem to present him to the Lord." Luke 2:23 says, "As it is written in the law of the Lord, every firstborn male shall be designated as holy to the Lord." Luke 2:24 says, "Joseph and Mary offered a sacrifice according to what is stated in the law of the Lord." Luke 2:27 says that Joseph and Mary brought Jesus to the temple "to do for him what was customary under the law." Luke 2:39 says that Joseph and Mary took Jesus home to Nazareth "when they had finished everything required by the law of the Lord." Five times in eighteen verses Luke mentions the fact that what Joseph and Mary did when Jesus was born, they did as an observant Jewish family out of faithful obedience to the law of Moses.

Luke's words, which so clearly identify Jesus within Judaism, confront us with the vast distance between Luke chapter two and the year two thousand, when some people believe that Christians who follow Jesus and Jews who embrace Judaism are not only separate from, but are opposed to, one another. That perception has grown large across the twenty centuries that stretch between Luke two and two thousand. But that certainly does not reflect the truth that we encounter in Luke 2. Something must have gone wrong, somewhere between Luke two and two thousand. The truth is, when Jesus was born in the manger, he was a Jew, and when he died on the cross, he was still a Jew, as were most of his followers. And even after he was crucified and resurrected, his followers remained within Judaism. They did not immediately strike out to start a new religion called "Christianity"; rather, they started out as a new group within Judaism. That is where the church began—not as a new religion called "Christianity," but as a new movement within Judaism. (Our church, Northminster Baptist Church, in the days before we had a home, borrowed our worship space from Temple Beth Israel. Every church ought to start out in a synagogue, because that is exactly where the church got its start, within Judaism!)

But somehow something went wrong. Somewhere between Luke two and two thousand, we Christians began to act toward Jews in ways that utterly, totally, and completely deny the spirit of Jesus. In 388, Christians in Callinicus, a town on the Euphrates, attacked and burned a synagogue. Their bishop led them in their violence. In 414, Christians destroyed the Jewish settlement in Alexandria, Egypt, again by violent assault. In the late eleventh century, Christian crusaders broke into the synagogue at Trier and destroyed the

Torah scrolls. In 1391, Jews in Seville, Barcelona, and Valencia were attacked by Christians incited to riot by a Christian preacher named Ferrant Martinez. Hitler's forced gathering of Jews into "ghettos" that marked the horrors of the Holocaust was pre-dated by a 16th-century Papal decree that established an area to which Jews must be restricted.[2] All of this is not to suggest that all Christians participated in these horrors and that no Christians protested against them. But it is to say that something went awfully, terribly wrong. Christians, supposedly acting in the name of Christ, who was himself a Jew, assaulted Jews in an effort to force them to convert to Christianity. Few threads in the fabric of human history are darker or stranger or sadder than that tragic line that has woven its way across the centuries. Our sins against the Jews are without excuse. For all those sins, I ask, in this Christian book, for the forgiveness of God and the forgiveness of God's children, the Jews.

It is a fierce irony that the very One who seems to divide Christians from Judaism, Jesus, is the One who forever binds Christians to Judaism because he himself was a Jew, not only when he cried in the cradle but also when he died on the cross. We are not only bound to the Jews by Jesus' human life within Judaism, but we are also bound to the Jews by the fact that we and they are all a part of the one great story of God. The Jesus we follow did not come into the world to reveal some new character development in an evolving God, but to reveal the one, eternal God of Abraham, Isaac, and Jacob in a clearer, fuller, nearer way. We are all bound up in the same story. There aren't two Gods, one Old Testament and the other New Testament. There is just this one God, most fully revealed in Jesus, the Jew who came preaching the gospel of God as the Son of God.

I have long struggled with all of this. It has taken me "all my life up to now" to speak the truth about all of this. Even as a child, I felt this mystical, spiritual bond to the people of God called the Jews. Yet, the religion of my youth taught me to make the harshest of all final judgments about the Jews because they do not name Jesus as Messiah. Then, one day, I attended a service of worship in a Jewish temple, where people of God offered prayers to the God of Abraham, Isaac, and Jacob, the God to whom Jesus prayed, the God to whom I, and all other Christians, pray. Later that day, alone in my home, I stared out a window at the setting sun and I said to God, "I know what I was taught to believe about the Jews, but I can't believe it. I don't have a new belief to replace it; all I know is that I don't believe the old belief." It was a moment of truth. (You can be honest with God. The sky won't fall.)

But what about Acts chapter four? Isn't that where Peter said, "This Jesus is the stone that was rejected by your builders . . . There is salvation in no one else, for there is no other name under heaven given among mortals by which we must be saved"? That is indeed what Peter said in Acts 4:12. But the same Bible that gives us Acts 4:12 also gives us Luke 10:25-28, which says, "Just then, a lawyer stood up to test Jesus. 'Teacher,' he said, 'what must I do to inherit eternal life?' Jesus said to him, 'What is written in the law? What do you read there?' He answered, 'You shall love the Lord your God with all your heart, and with all your soul, and with all your strength, and with all your mind; and your neighbor as yourself.' And Jesus said to him, 'You have given the right answer; do this, and you will live.'" Because we read the Bible through the lens of our assumptions, we might have expected Jesus to respond to the inquirer's request for the way to eternal life by saying, "Invite me into your heart" or "Accept me as your Savior." But to read the Bible and speak the truth is to confess that Jesus told this seeker fully to embrace his Judaism as the way to eternal life. What one makes of that may be debatable, but the fact that it is so is inarguably true.

But what about John fourteen? Isn't that where Jesus said, "I am the way, the truth and the life. No one comes to the Father but by me"? Indeed, Jesus did say exactly that. To read the Bible and speak the truth is to acknowledge that Jesus said *exactly* that. Jesus didn't say, "I have come to start a new world religion called Christianity which will be the way, the truth, and the life." Nor did he say, "No one comes to the Father but by Christian doctrine." What he said was, "I am the way, the truth, and the life. No one comes to the Father but by me." We have assumed that we know what that means. Perhaps our assumption is correct, but let's be honest. Our assumption is based on someone's interpretation of John 14 and not on the stark, bare, unadorned words of John 14.

But what about Romans nine through eleven? Isn't that where Paul, speaking of the Jews who rejected Jesus as Messiah, says, "I have great sorrow in my heart, for I wish that I myself were accursed for the sake of my own people, the Israelites"? That is what Paul says, at the *beginning* of his long, arduous passage. But at the *end* of the passage, near the conclusion of chapter 11, this is what Paul says: "All Israel will be saved . . . For God has included all in disobedience so that God may be merciful to all." What does that mean? Who can say? Apparently, not even Paul, because it is at that point that Paul lapses into a song over the mystery of it all. As soon as he says, "God has included all in disobedience so that God may be merciful to all," he sings, "O the depth of the riches and wisdom and knowledge of God! How unsearchable are God's judgments!" Once Paul has said all he knows to say, he casts us all, Jews and non-Jews, on the mercy of God. And then he lapses into a doxology to the wonder and mystery of the ways of God with people. Paul sings, at last, of the mystery of mercy. But his word to us, in the midst of it all, is clear. He says to us, the non-Jews who have chosen to follow Jesus, in Romans 11:17: "You, the church, are the wild olive branches, grafted to the rich root

(Judaism) . . . It is not you that supports the root, but the root (Judaism) that supports you (the church) . . . So do not become proud, but stand in awe." "Stand in awe," Paul says to we who are Christians. Stand in awe that you get to be a part of what started with Abraham. Stand in awe of the fact that the One who was born to Mary at Bethlehem, himself a Jew, has opened the way for those of you who are not Jews to know God. Stand in awe of the fact that you, who are not Jews, even get to be included.

That is not unlike what Simeon said, back in Luke 2. Simeon took Jesus from Mary, held him in his arms, and said, "This is the one who has come to bring the light to the Gentiles and to Israel." We were together then, back in Luke 2, and we are still together in the great heart of God. We are bound to one another in ways that none of us can fully comprehend this side of heaven, where God waits in mercy.

It is very important for us to read the Bible and then speak the truth about what we have found there concerning Judaism and Christianity. Let us speak the truth. The truth is, Judaism and Christianity are distinct and particular from one another in ways that should never be minimalized or trivialized. The truth is, neither Judaism nor Christianity benefits from a blurring of the decisive differences that distinguish one faith from the other. The truth is, it isn't easy or simple to reconcile all that we find in Scripture about Judaism and Jesus and emerging Christianity; indeed, it sometimes seems well-nigh impossible. All of this is true. But the truth that rings truest of all is this: We who follow Jesus were together with the Jews at the house of God in Luke two, and we are together with the Jews in the heart of God in two thousand.

Thanks be to God, the God of Abraham, Isaac, Jacob, and Jesus.

Amen.

* * * * *

I am a Jew, born and raised in a Christian country. Jesus has been a part of my mental world since I was old enough to think. On the one hand, I have always found him an enormously attractive figure, challenging and inspiring. On the other . . . When I was little, growing up in a mixed Jewish-Catholic neighborhood, most of my playmates were Italian-American boys. They were friends, but I learned to stay in my own house on Good Friday, since after hearing the sermon at [their] church, some of them would come looking for me to punish me for killing Christ. Once they caught me out on the street and knocked me down. "But Jesus was a Jew!" I shouted through my tears. That idea, which they had never contemplated, infuriated them. It earned me a few extra kicks and punches.

—*Richard E. Rubenstein,*
When Jesus Became God

NOTE

[1] Edward Cohen, *The Peddler's Grandson* (Jackson: University Press of Mississippi, 1999), 49.

[2] A comprehensive record of Christianity and anti-Semitism can be found in James Carroll, *Constantine's Sword* (New York: Houghton Mifflin Co., 2001).

CHAPTER TWENTY-ONE

The Gospel of God

> Now after John was arrested, Jesus came to Galilee, pro-
> claiming the gospel of God, and saying, "The time is
> fulfilled, and the kingdom of God has come near; repent,
> and believe in the good news."
>
> —*Mark 1:14-15*

The gospel of Mark places in our path this enormous little
phrase, "the gospel of God." Mark 1:14 summarizes Jesus' life
and work with that wonderful sentence, "Jesus came preaching
the gospel of God." When I use the word "gospel," I am
almost always thinking of Christianity, of the New Testament,
of what we most often call "the gospel of Jesus Christ." It is
hard for me to remember that when Jesus came preaching the
gospel, it was not the gospel of a religion called "Christianity"
because, in the lifetime of Jesus, Christianity did not exist.
Nor was it the gospel of the New Testament, because there was
no New Testament. It was, as Mark tells us, the gospel of God
that Jesus came preaching. That gospel of God was the good
story about the way God really is, and it was the same story
that had always been true about God.

The life of Jesus was the ultimate revelation of the gospel of God, but the Old Testament is filled with glimpses of the gospel of God. Even all the way back in the time of Noah, there was this good news about God. When the flood was over and the ark had landed, God was so grieved about the flood's destruction that God promised never to do it again. God even went so far as to hang out rainbows as a reminder that God had promised never again to be provoked by God's children into such a destructive response. God said, "As for me, I'm never going to do this again." And with that great promise of mercy and grace, we get an early glimpse of the gospel of God. As the centuries unfold, God has many opportunities to keep that promise because God's patience is tried many times. Over and over, God's people fail God's hopes and neglect God's call and ignore God's love, but over and over God will not let them go. This is the gospel of God, and it is nowhere more powerfully captured than in that great corner of the Old Testament where God, through the prophet Hosea, says:

> When Israel was a child, I loved her and I called her out of Egypt, but the more I called them, the more they went away from me . . . But how can I give them up? My heart recoils within me; my compassion grows warm and tender. I will not execute my fierce anger, for I am God, and not human . . . I am the Holy One and I will not come in wrath . . . I will heal their disloyalty. I will love them freely, for my anger has turned from them. I will be like the dew to Israel . . . They shall live again beneath my shadow. They shall flourish as a garden and blossom like a vine. (Hos 11 and 14)

That is a grand glimpse of the gospel of God, the same gospel of God that Jesus came to reveal in its clearest, fullest, most complete revelation.